EYE ON
Art

IMPRESSIONISM

EYE ON
Art

IMPRESSIONISM

by Peggy J. Parks

LUCENT BOOKS

An imprint of Thomson Gale, a part of The Thomson Corporation

THOMSON
✦
GALE

Detroit • New York • San Francisco • New Haven, Conn. • Waterville, Maine • London

THOMSON

GALE

™

© 2007 Thomson Gale, a part of The Thomson Corporation.

Thomson and Star Logo are trademarks and Gale and Lucent Books are registered trademarks used herein under license.

For more information, contact
Lucent Books
27500 Drake Rd.
Farmington Hills, MI 48331-3535
Or you can visit our Internet site at http://www.gale.com

LIBRARY OF CONGRESS CATALOGING-IN-PUBLICATION DATA

Parks, Peggy J., 1951–
Impressionism / by Peggy J. Parks.
    p. cm. — (Eye on art)
Includes bibliographical references.
ISBN-13: 978-1-59018-958-0 (hardcover : alk. paper)
ISBN-10: 1-59018-958-2 (hardcover : alk. paper)
1. Impressionism (Art)—France—Juvenile literature. 2. Painting,
French—19th century—Juvenile literature. 3. Impressionist artists—France—Juvenile
literature. I. Title.

ND547.5.I4P374 2006
759.4'09034--dc22

2006018521

Printed in the United States of America

CONTENTS

Foreword

Some thirty-one thousand years ago, early humans painted strikingly sophisticated images of horses, bison, rhinoceroses, bears, and other animals on the walls of a cave in southern France. The meaning of these elaborate pictures is unknown, although some experts speculate that they held ceremonial significance. Regardless of their intended purpose, the Chauvet-Pont-d'Arc cave paintings represent some of the first known expressions of the artistic impulse.

From the Paleolithic era to the present day, human beings have continued to create works of visual art. Artists have developed painting, drawing, sculpture, engraving, and many other techniques to produce visual representations of landscapes, the human form, religious and historical events, and countless other subjects. The artistic impulse also finds expression in glass, jewelry, and new forms inspired by new technology. Indeed, judging by humanity's prolific artistic output throughout history, one must conclude that the compulsion to produce art is an inherent aspect of being human, and the results are among humanity's greatest cultural achievements: masterpieces such as the architectural marvels of ancient Greece, Michelangelo's perfectly rendered statue *David*, Vincent van Gogh's visionary painting *Starry Night*, and endless other treasures.

The creative impulse serves many purposes for society. At its most basic level, art is a form of entertainment or the means for a satisfying or pleasant aesthetic experience. But art's true power lies not in its potential to entertain and delight but in its ability to enlighten, to reveal the truth, and by doing so to uplift the human spirit and transform the human race.

One of the primary functions of art has been to serve religion. For most of Western history, for example, artists were paid by the church to produce works with religious themes and subjects. Art was thus a tool to help human beings transcend mundane, secular reality and achieve spiritual enlightenment. One of the best-known, and largest-scale, examples of Christian religious art is the Sistine Chapel in the Vatican in Rome. In 1508 Pope Julius II commissioned Italian Renaissance artist Michelangelo to paint the chapel's vaulted ceiling, an area of 640 square yards (535 sq. m). Michelangelo spent four years on scaffolding, his neck craned, creating a panoramic fresco of some three hundred human figures. His paintings depict Old Testament prophets and heroes, sibyls of Greek mythology, and nine scenes from the Book of Genesis, including the Creation of Adam, the Fall of Adam and Eve from the Garden of Eden, and the Flood. The ceiling of the Sistine Chapel is considered one of the greatest works of Western art and has inspired the awe of countless Christian pilgrims and other religious seekers. As eighteenth-century German poet and author Johann Wolfgang von Goethe wrote, "Until you have seen this Sistine Chapel, you can have no adequate conception of what man is capable of."

In addition to inspiring religious fervor, art can serve as a force for social change. Artists are among the visionaries of any culture. As such, they often perceive injustice and wrongdoing and confront others by reflecting what they see in their work. One classic example of art as social commentary was created in May 1937, during the brutal Spanish civil war. On May 1 Spanish artist Pablo Picasso learned of the recent attack on the small Basque village of Guernica by German airplanes allied with fascist forces led by Francisco Franco. The German pilots had used the village for target practice, a three-hour bombing that killed sixteen hundred civilians. Picasso, living in Paris, channeled his outrage over the massacre into his painting *Guernica*, a black, white, and gray mural that depicts dismembered animals and fractured human figures whose faces are contorted in agonized expressions. Initially, critics and the public condemned the painting as an incoherent hodgepodge, but the work soon came to be seen as a powerful antiwar statement and remains an iconic symbol of the violence and terror that dominated world events during the remainder of the twentieth century.

The impulse to create art—whether painting animals with crude pigments on a cave wall, sculpting a human form from marble, or commemorating human tragedy in a mural—thus serves many purposes. It offers an entertaining diversion, nourishes the imagination and the spirit, decorates and beautifies the world, and chronicles the age. But underlying all these functions is the desire to reveal that which is obscure— to illuminate, clarify, and perhaps ennoble. As Picasso himself stated, "The purpose of art is washing the dust of daily life off our souls."

The Eye on Art series is intended to assist readers in understanding the various roles of art in society. Each volume offers an in-depth exploration of a major artistic movement, medium, figure, or profession. All books in the series are beautifully illustrated with full-color photographs and diagrams. Riveting narrative, clear technical explanation, informative sidebars, fully documented quotes, a bibliography, and a thorough index all provide excellent starting points for research and discussion. With these features, the Eye on Art series is a useful introduction to the world of art—a world that can offer both insight and inspiration.

Introduction

"It Is Shocking . . . Complete Craziness"

Few artistic movements in history have provoked as intense a reaction, or been as influential, as the nineteenth-century genre known as Impressionism. Art historian Michael Wilson describes the enduring allure of the paintings created by the movement's French founders in his book, *The Impressionists*: "Their devotion to the beauties of the everyday scene has given their pictures a lasting attraction; so appealing is the freshness of colour, the liveliness of technique, that it is easy to forget how long ago they were painted."[1] Today, people who have an appreciation for fine art gaze in awe at the masterpieces that were created by the Impressionist artists—yet they may not know how much those painters suffered for their efforts as they resolved to create their own, individual style of art.

Origins

The Impressionist movement began during the mid-1800s, when Paris was considered the artistic capital of Europe. In Parisian society, painting was a subject of great interest and a popular topic of discussion among the middle and upper classes. At the time, the art establishment was dominated by an organization known as the Académie des Beaux-Arts (Academy of Fine Arts), which had existed since the 1600s.

The masters of the Académie set the standards for French art by determining what types of paintings were acceptable, which were almost exclusively limited to religious scenes, mythology, significant historical themes, and portraits of heroes and other influential people. Art historian E.H. Gombrich describes the profound impact these rigid expectations had on painters of the day: "It is curious how rarely artists before the middle of the eighteenth century strayed from these narrow limits of illustration, how rarely they painted a scene from a romance, or an episode of medieval or contemporary history."[2] In addition to dictating appropriate subject matter, the Académie also had expectations for the techniques artists should use, such as painting in somber, conservative tones rather than broad or bright palettes, using symmetrical compositions and hard outlines, and creating meticulously smooth surfaces that showed virtually no trace of brushstrokes.

Salon de Paris art exhibitions were held at the Palais des Beaux-Arts (pictured) every two years.

The Académie's prestigious art exhibition, the Salon de Paris, was held every two years until 1863, when it became an annual event. Only art that was selected by the Salon jury could be displayed, and for the artists who were chosen, there were numerous benefits. Young, unknown painters whose works were accepted by the jury had the coveted opportunity to display their artistic creations alongside established, reputable masters to an audience that numbered in the thousands. In many cases, these budding artists could win medals, prizes, and even large cash commissions, as well as gain fame and recognition for their work. Of course, most artists wanted the Académie's endorsement and craved the ability to display their paintings publicly, so they adhered to the organization's rules—until a group of young, daring, and highly talented French painters shocked the art world by creating a radically different style of art that later became known as Impressionism.

The artists who dared to defy the establishment banded together during the last half of the nineteenth century because they shared a common goal: painting the way they wanted to instead of obeying the archaic and restrictive rules that had been forced on artists for years. Even though they had great respect for classical paintings and the artists who created them, they rejected the practice of painting based on firm, traditional rules. Rather, the Impressionists wanted to paint exactly what they saw firsthand, looking at each subject anew, as if they were seeing it for the very first time.

Breaking the Rules of Art

The paintings by the Impressionists were different from anything that had ever been created before, and they broke all the rules that artists had adhered to for generations. Unlike traditional artists who covered their canvases with a dark undercoat before they began painting, the Impressionists painted on white or cream-colored backgrounds to achieve a lighter, brighter effect. Their paintings featured clear tones and pure, unblended colors; feathery brushstrokes that captured the essence of a subject, rather than the details; and paint that was

applied so thickly the texture of the finished work was rough, rather than smooth and polished. Master Impressionist Claude Monet once described this style of painting to a fellow artist: "When you go out to paint, try to forget what objects you have before you, a tree, a house, a field, or whatever. Merely think, here is a little square of blue, here is an oblong of pink, here is a streak of yellow, and paint it just as it looks to you, the exact color and shape, until it gives you your own naive impression of the scene before you."[3] Another consistent feature of Impressionism was the way the artists intentionally emphasized natural light, reflections, and shadows in their paintings.

The Impressionists' daring, unprecedented approach to painting certainly captured attention—but initially, that attention constituted scorn and disgust rather than any sort of appreciation. After all, the artists had tossed aside hundreds of years of accepted painting methods, and in doing so, they infuriated the establishment, prompting well-known art critics and journalists to chastise them publicly for creating art that was considered nothing short of scandalous. One of those critics,

King Charles X presents awards to the artists at the end of the Salon de Paris exhibition in 1824.

BIEN FÉROCE!

Les Turcs achetant plusieurs toiles à l'Exposition des impressionnistes
pour s'en servir en cas de guerre.

This cartoon portrays the Impressionists' paintings as so awful that they could be used to scare off an enemy.

Albert Wolff, expressed his distaste in a publication called *Le Figaro* in the year 1874: "It is shocking to see how human vanity can lose itself in complete craziness. Try once to make it clear to Mr. Pissarro [Impressionist painter] that branches are not violet, that the sky does not have the colour of fresh butter, that one cannot see anywhere in the world the things which he paints and that no intelligent person can take such discrepancies seriously."[4]

Numerous people who were influential in the artistic establishment shared Wolff's perspective about this radical style of painting. As a result, the Impressionists suffered ridicule and rejection for many years. Ironically, the work of these artists who were disrespected, even shunned, in their own time is immensely popular today, as Gombrich explains:

The critics who had laughed had proved very fallible indeed. Had they bought these canvases rather than mocked them they would have become rich. Criticism therefore suffered a loss of prestige from which it never recovered. The struggle of the Impressionists became the treasured legend of all innovators in art, who could always point to this conspicuous failure of the public to recognize novel methods. In a sense this notorious failure is as important in the history of art as was the ultimate victory of the Impressionist programme.[5]

The movement started by the Impressionists became a powerful force in the artistic world—and in the process, it changed the nature of art forever.

The Roots of Impressionism

Although the development of Impressionism actually began in the mid-1800s, the foundation for new types of art had been established many years before that. An early contributing factor was the volatile political climate in Europe, especially in France. The painters who inspired and influenced Impressionist artists lived during a period of major political and social upheaval. The French Revolution of 1789, as well as the restless years before the rise of Napoléon, France's emperor, set a pattern of political unrest and constitutional change. This was the catalyst for the development of more progressive thinking and radical ideas, including approaches to art that were very different from what the establishment liked or was willing to accept.

One of the predecessors of Impressionism was Romanticism, an artistic and intellectual movement that began in the late eighteenth century. Romanticism, which was characterized by the favoring of emotion and imagination over reason and of the senses over knowledge, rebelled against established social rules and conventions. Art historian Robert Cumming describes the movement and explains how it influenced art:

Heroic individualism defined Romanticism. It also marked a decisive break with the conformities of the past. . . . The desire to see everything as larger than life frequently expressed itself in bold color, vigorous brushwork, and themes of love, death, heroism, and the wonders of nature. . . . Heightened emotions dominated. Artists turned away from the logical and rational, allowing themselves freedom to express raw, usually suppressed feelings. Movement, color, and drama were actively championed, exoticism favored.[6]

Capturing Natural Beauty

Cumming's reference to nature is significant because an important element of Romanticism was a deepened appreciation of natural beauty. This led to the increased popularity of painting landscapes, which was a definite change from traditional artistic conventions. Up until that point, the Académie des Beaux-Arts considered most landscape painting to be a minor, if not slightly inferior, genre of art. Almost all reputable artists worked in studios, where they painted portraits, religious scenes, or other similar subjects using artificial light. The artists who earned their livings painting pastoral scenes, country estates, or picturesque scenery were not typically taken seriously by their peers or by the establishment. But by the end of the eighteenth century, that attitude began to change. More and more artists started painting in a style known as *plein air* (meaning "outdoors"), so they could capture the qualities and sensations of being outside in the open air, using natural light.

At first, landscape painting was more popular with artists in Great Britain than in France. One British artist, John Constable, was especially fond of painting the countryside near his London home. Constable was a deeply spiritual man who was passionate about the beauty of nature. He loved to paint the effects of changing light on his canvas, as well as the shifting patterns of clouds as they drifted across the sky. And while he painted years before the Impressionist movement began, some of his artistic techniques could definitely be considered Impressionistic.

Constable, for instance, shunned the traditional finished looks that were favored by other landscape artists, and instead focused on making his paintings look more realistic. To depict weather changes and flickering sunlight, he used blobs of white or yellow paint on the canvas, and to capture the drama of storms, he applied rapid, bold brushstrokes. It was Constable's goal to paint exactly what he saw, rather than using the formulaic, predictable color schemes and techniques that were so common among other landscape artists. "There is room enough for a natural painter," he once wrote to a friend. "The great vice of the present day is [showiness], an attempt to do something beyond the truth."[7]

Although Constable was well known as a landscape artist, he was not particularly successful in his native England. In France, however, he achieved artistic credibility as well as fame. His painting entitled *The Hay Wain* was accepted for

John Constable's *The Hay Wain* inspired other painters, including French landscape artist Eugène Delacroix.

Eugène Delacroix

Ferdinand-Victor-Eugène Delacroix was born on April 26, 1798, in Charenton-Saint Maurice, near Paris. He studied under the French painter Pierre Guérin, who trained his young student in the classical style of artist Jacques-Louis David, although an even stronger influence on Delacroix was the colorful, opulent style of master painters Peter Paul Rubens and Paolo Veronese. Delacroix's technique of applying contrasting colors with small strokes of his brush to create a vibrant, dramatic effect on the canvas was an inspiration for the Impressionist artists.

Delacroix's artistic career began in 1822, when his first painting, *The Barque of Dante,* was accepted for display at the Salon, but the true catalyst of his fame was his 1824 masterpiece, *Massacre at Chios.* By the 1830s, he had become known as the undisputed leader of the Romantic movement, a distinction he held throughout his life. Toward the end of his career, he was so highly respected that he often received lucrative commissions to paint murals and ceiling designs in government buildings. Delacroix died in Paris on August 13, 1863.

Massacre at Chios was nearly finished when Eugène Delacroix decided to rework it.

exhibition at the Salon in 1824 and was awarded a prestigious gold medal by the Académie. Years later, his paintings, as well as those of other British landscape artists, became an inspiration for French painters. They, too, decided to leave their studios and venture outdoors, where they could capture the beauty of natural surroundings and the changing moods of light. Art historian Wynford Dewhurst explained this in his 1904 book, *Impressionist Painting*: "The influence of these Englishmen upon French painting during the nineteenth century is one of the most striking episodes in the history of art. They were animated by a new spirit, the spirit of sincerity and truth. The French landscape group . . . was the direct result of Constable's power."[8]

One of the French landscape artists who was inspired and influenced by Constable was Eugène Delacroix. After seeing *The Hay Wain* in Paris in 1824, he was captivated by Constable's use of brilliant color in the sky, trees, pastures, and water. Delacroix was so impressed with these techniques that he decided to rework a painting of his own entitled *Massacre at Chios*, even though he had almost finished the piece. In an effort to emulate the artistic effects he so admired, Delacroix added glaze to his painting, as well as thick patches of pure pigment in a variety of vivid colors. From that point on, he became known for his use of expressive color and movement, as well as his fierce devotion to creating paintings that looked natural. Like Constable before him, Delacroix was passionate about capturing the constantly changing qualities of light and color because, as he once said, in the natural world "light and shadow never stand still."[9]

The Barbizon School

Constable and Delacroix served as mentors for other artists who desired to break away from established artistic traditions. They, too, wanted to paint landscapes in their purely natural state, using expressive colors and highlighting the sunlight as it danced across the land. Beginning in the late 1830s, a group of these artists started gathering in the French village of

Barbizon, which was surrounded by the picturesque forest of Fontainebleau. This group of like-minded painters—among them Théodore Rousseau, Charles-François Daubigny, Constant Troyon, Jean-François Millet, and Jean-Baptiste-Camille Corot—lived and worked in Barbizon, and eventually became known as the Barbizon school.

Away from their studios and the rigors of hectic city life, the artists found fresh inspiration in the peaceful, quiet forest. And while each produced works in his own individual style, they all shared a fascination with the natural beauty surrounding them. They painted landscapes that reflected the dramatic effects of dawn and dusk, as well as the breathtaking beauty of the changing seasons, and by doing so, they significantly influenced artistic trends.

Corot, one of the leaders of the Barbizon school, was especially fond of painting outside in bright sunlight. His home

Jean-François Millet wanted his paintings to communicate the realistic aspects of life, but *The Gleaners* was interpreted as a social protest.

was in Paris, but during the warm months of the year, he often traveled throughout France, England, Switzerland, and Italy, where he observed and painted the rural countryside. On one of his trips to Italy, Corot wrote a letter to his parents saying that he had only one goal in life, and that was to paint landscapes. Art historian Guy Jennings describes him as "a respected elder statesman of French painting, a serene but notable influence [whose] gift to the new avant-garde was a sense of light and landscape unequalled by any of his contemporaries."[10]

Yet even though Corot's greatest love was painting natural scenery, he still conformed to artistic practices that were deemed worthy by the establishment. He sought the Académie's approval because he wanted to display his work at the Salon. As a result, the paintings he created for public exhibition were not as vividly colorful—nor nearly as bold—as those he created for private display in his own personal studio. Like most landscape artists of his time, Corot generally depicted lovely, peaceful scenes that were beautiful and pleasing to the eye. That was one reason why the Académie continued to hold him in high regard, and the jury regularly accepted the paintings he submitted.

The Dawn of Realism

Jean-François Millet, another founder of the Barbizon school, was more daring than Corot. Millet also painted peaceful outdoor scenes, but he expanded his works to include people, and the subjects he painted were not appealing to the artistic establishment. Rather than depicting prominent citizens, heroic figures, or other subjects that were deemed acceptable, Millet painted common, hardworking people who were struggling to get through their daily lives. He found it disturbing that even though it was the industrial age, living conditions had increasingly deteriorated for poor people. In 1857, Millet created a painting called *The Gleaners*, which featured three peasant women working in a field where harvesting was in progress. The painting was radically different from the exaggerated idealism of Romantic art and featured a realistic depiction of life as it truly was for those who were less fortunate. *The Gleaners* was interpreted as a social protest, but that was not Millet's intention when he painted it. He wanted only to create art that communicated life exactly as he saw it, showing ordinary people and events as they were, in an unglamorous, realistic manner. This style of painting eventually came to be known as Realism.

Gustave Courbet was another Realist artist who shared Millet's belief that paintings should depict the truth, but he took the idea much further. Courbet was a rebellious artist, someone who was deeply disturbed by the inequities and injustices of society. He was passionate about creating art that was brutally honest, and he believed this should be the mission of other Realist painters as well, as author William C. Seitz explains: "Courbet's theoretical principles . . . included abandonment of the imaginary and abstract subjects of Romanticism . . . in favor of scenes of contemporary life. He further insisted that the painter should represent only actual, existing, visible, and tangible objects, and these without the slightest imaginative alteration or idealization."[11]

Art Should Convey Truth

Courbet began creating his revolutionary works years before Millet and was credited with starting the Realist movement. His artwork was clearly defiant, intentionally flouting the idealistic nature of Romantic art. To convey irregularities in nature, as well as the harshness and cruelties of life, he painted spontaneous, rough brushstrokes on the canvas using thick paint. Courbet had no interest whatsoever in creating art that was considered pretty. Rather, he wanted only to convey reality, as he once explained to a friend: "I hope always to earn my living by my art without having ever deviated by even a hair's breadth from my principles, without having lied to my conscience for a single moment, without painting even as much as can be covered by a hand only to please anyone or to sell more easily."[12] As a result of his boldness, Courbet was often accused by art critics of being vulgar and of deliberately using his paintings to communicate a sense of ugliness.

As radical as Courbet's paintings were, however, the Académie still believed them to be worthy of endorsement. Several of his works were exhibited at the Paris Salon in 1850, the most provocative of which was entitled *Burial at Ornans.* Courbet had painted it from memory based on what he had seen at the funeral of his uncle two years before, and the finished product was enormous, measuring 10 by 22 feet (3m by 6.7m).

Even more startling than the painting's large size was the way Courbet had presented his subject matter, affording as much dignity to a common citizen's funeral as would be expected for the funeral of royalty. That was considered brash, as well as highly inappropriate, and art critics were shocked and outraged—but the public's reaction was just the opposite. People viewed Courbet's paintings, especially *Burial at Ornans,* as a rejection of the lavish, decadent idealism of the Romantic era. They found the work refreshing, a response to their need for art that was real, rather than contrived, and they embraced the painter who was daring enough to create it. Not only did *Burial at Ornans* help propel Courbet to fame, it also enhanced the popularity of Realism. Even more significantly, it marked the beginning of the end for Romanticism.

Although art critics were shocked and outraged by Gustave Courbet's *Burial at Ornans,* the public found it refreshing.

PORTABLE PAINT

Early nineteenth-century artists who wanted to paint landscapes made sketches outdoors, and then finished the paintings in their studios. Working outside was difficult because paint was not portable—artists had to grind and mix their own pigments with oil, and then store the mixed paints in small pouches. When they were ready to use their paints, they punched holes in the pouches and squeezed the paint onto their palettes. This was a challenge because once the pouch was opened, the paint had to be used up quickly or it would spoil.

That changed in 1841, when a new invention revolutionized the way artists stored and used paints. John Goffe Rand, an American artist living in London, invented the collapsible metal paint tube, and the idea was quickly adopted by merchants who sold the ready-to-use paints to artists. Encased in metal tubes similar to today's toothpaste tubes, the paint could be preserved much longer. That meant artists could use their paints for extended periods of time, no matter where they wanted to work. Also, the ability to purchase paint in tubes provided artists with another advantage: a selection of brilliant colors they had never had access to before.

"The Master of the Sky"

In 1859, Courbet became acquainted with another French Realist painter, Eugène Boudin, and the two soon became good friends. Courbet had great admiration for Boudin's talent and was particularly enthusiastic about the artist's brilliant seascapes. The son of a sailor, Boudin had spent his entire life around the ocean. At a young age, he had moved with his family to Le Havre, a seaport village in northern France, where he later went to work as a stationer's apprentice. As often as possible, he spent time outdoors pursuing his favorite hobbies of drawing and painting.

When Boudin was twenty years old, he left his job and opened his own stationery and picture framing shop, which allowed him to meet artists who worked in the area during the summer months. One of his customers was Jean-François Millet, who encouraged Boudin and offered helpful advice about his painting, but who was also completely honest with the budding artist about the difficulties of trying to make a living as a painter. Boudin loved art so much that he was willing to take the risk, and at the age of twenty-two, he sold his shop and devoted himself full-time to painting.

Boudin's greatest passion was working outside where he could capture the breathtaking beauty of the sea, beaches, and sky. For days on end, he worked tirelessly in front of his canvas at the harbor, on the beach, and on the local cliffs. He painted at all times of the year, in a variety of changing light and weather conditions, and eventually became revered for his stunning seascapes. Corot, himself a master of plein air painting, once expressed his admiration for Boudin by telling him, "You are the master of the sky."[13]

A Most Influential Artist

Of the many painters who, like Boudin, were instrumental in ushering in the era of Impressionism, by far the most influential was Édouard Manet. An artist in the Realist style, Manet was a great admirer of Tiziano Vecelli (commonly known as Titian), Diego Velázquez, Francisco Goya, and the other beloved European painters who were known as the old masters. These artists' paintings were housed at the famed Louvre in Paris, as well as at museums in other major European cities, and Manet spent untold hours studying and meticulously copying them.

Yet as much as Manet admired the works of the masters, he shared the beliefs of Charles Baudelaire, an influential and outspoken writer who urged painters to create art that depicted contemporary life. Manet painted everyday subjects and events such as café scenes, Spanish dancers, parties, and bull-fights, as well as scenery in both urban and suburban settings. His paintings often featured strong outlines, rough brush-strokes, and harsh contrasts, which resulted in works that were rich and elegant, as Cumming explains: "He was unique in that he had a brilliant, very visual and sketchy painting technique, involving the use of large areas of flat color. Has anyone ever used black so lusciously and with such visual impact?"[14]

Manet craved the Académie's acceptance, and his greatest desire was to be thought of as the modern successor of the old masters. But that was not to be, as his style of art was considered peculiar at best, and in some cases nothing short of shameful. In 1859, the Salon jury rejected *Absinthe Drinker*, the first painting Manet had submitted for exhibition. Two years later, when the jury accepted two of his other paintings, he saw this as a promising sign—but his enthusiasm was short-lived. In the following years, the jury rarely accepted his works, and Manet became bitterly disappointed over what he perceived to be a blatant and intentional snub.

Manet was not hesitant to express his feelings, more than once complaining publicly about how he was being abused. As a result, he developed a reputation as a troublemaker and a rebel. But even that did not change his belief that artists should establish a good rapport with the Académie and seek to exhibit their works at the Salon, as he later wrote: "Monsieur Manet . . . has no intention of overthrowing old methods of painting, or creating new ones. He has merely tried to be himself, and nobody else."[15]

Rejection and Rebellion

In 1863, the jury rejected another painting Manet had submitted for Salon exhibition, and its provocative subject matter reinforced the artistic establishment's negative opinion of him. Entitled *Déjeuner sur l'Herbe* (*Luncheon on the Grass*), the painting featured a young woman who was completely nude, casually enjoying a picnic in the company of two fully clothed men. In addition to viewing the painting as a shameful and indecent piece of pornography, the jury was equally appalled at Manet's artistic techniques of applying paint to the canvas in broad swaths and using fragmented colors to simulate flickering sunlight.

Manet was disappointed and angry at the jury's refusal to accept *Déjeuner sur l'Herbe*—yet his rejection was just one of thousands that occurred that year. In 1863 alone, of the five thousand paintings that were submitted for Salon exhibition, more than half of the works were rejected by the jury, including one that had been commissioned by the wife of the French emperor Napoléon III. Artists had finally had enough. For years they had endured the Académie's narrow-mindedness, arrogance, and prejudice, and they were determined to do something about it. Hundreds of them began expressing their outrage to the French government, and the emperor responded to their protests by agreeing to take action.

Critics dismissed Édouard Manet's artwork as peculiar and shameful.

On April 24, 1863, Napoléon III issued an official decree for an alternative exhibition to take place one month later. The event, known as the Salon des Refusés (Salon of the Refused), was held in the splendid Palais de l'Industrie, the same building that hosted the official Salon. Thousands of people attended, with most of them laughing and treating the exhibition as a joke. The artistic establishment was especially eager to hurl insults at paintings they considered unworthy of public display—but by far, the most scathing criticism was directed toward Manet's *Déjeuner sur l'Herbe*. Even Napoléon himself declared the painting to be a disgrace, and art critics everywhere viciously attacked it. One of those critics was Théophile Thoré, whose review appeared in the publication *Salons* following the exhibit. "Unfortunately," wrote Thoré, "the nude hasn't a good figure and one can't think of anything uglier than

Manet endured the most scathing criticism for *Déjeuner sur l'Herbe* (*Luncheon on the Grass*).

the man stretched out beside her, who hasn't even thought of taking off . . . his horrid padded cap. It is the contrast of a creature so inappropriate in a pastoral scene with this naked bather that is so shocking."[16]

The harsh criticism and blatant rebuff of his painting humiliated and angered Manet. But even in the face of public ridicule, he remained committed to creating art in his own way, rather than conforming to the artistic establishment's rigid expectations. Little did he know that in the following years, he would suffer even worse rejection. Nor could he have known that his radical beliefs would set off a firestorm of controversy in the artistic world, as well as pave the way for the development of a bold new genre of art known as Impressionism.

2

An Artistic Revolution

Although it was never Édouard Manet's intent to be a revolutionary, he was certainly viewed that way by the artistic establishment. But in the eyes of a group of young, free-thinking artists, he was a hero for refusing to back down when challenged and criticized. To them, Manet was a symbol of courage and strength, a mentor worthy of their admiration, as Michael Wilson explains: "It was to him that young painters now looked for leadership in the fight against the Academy and the Salon jury."[17] Inspired by Manet, these artists were naturally drawn together and developed a close friendship, as well as strong professional alliances with each other—and this alliance strengthened their resolve to strike out on their own and defy the rigidity of the artistic establishment.

Four of these progressive artists were Claude Monet, Pierre-Auguste Renoir, Jean-Frédéric Bazille, and Alfred Sisley. They had originally met in 1862 as students of Charles Gleyre, a Swiss painter who taught art classes in his Paris studio, known as an atelier. They were from very different backgrounds and social classes, but they shared a deep passion for art, as well as a burning desire to paint in their own individual styles. These four artists would eventually form the core group of the Impressionist movement.

Claude Monet

By the time Monet began his studies with Gleyre, he had a significant amount of experience with landscape painting. Born in Paris in November 1840 and raised in the seaport city of Le Havre, Monet had shown natural artistic talent at a very young age. He was an undisciplined, rebellious child who did not like to live by the rules, and to him, school was no better than a prison. He spent much of his class time doodling in the margins of his books and mocking his teachers by drawing caricatures of them, all the while gazing out the windows and dreaming of being outside. Whenever he could get away, he spent his hours sketching scenery at the beach, out on the towering cliffs, or in the harbor, as well as drawing caricatures of the people he observed in town.

Even before he was a teenager, Monet had developed a reputation as a gifted artist, and his drawings were being displayed in the window of a Le Havre picture framing shop. There he was introduced to master seascape painter Eugène Boudin, who offered some advice to the aspiring young artist. "You are gifted," Boudin told him, "one can see that at a glance. But I hope you are not going to stop at that . . . soon you will have had enough of caricaturing. . . . Study, learn to see and to paint, draw, make landscapes. They are all so beautiful, the sea and the sky, the animals, the people, and the trees, just as nature has made them with their character, their real way of being, in the light, in the air, just as they are."[18]

Monet had seen Boudin's nature paintings displayed in the shop window and he did not like them, nor did he have much interest in painting landscapes. As time went by, though, Boudin managed to persuade Monet to try painting outdoors, and the two often worked side by side at the seashore. Years later, Monet credited Boudin for broadening his artistic ability and encouraging him to be more creative and expressive. "Suddenly a veil was torn away," Monet wrote. "I had understood—I had realized what painting could be. By the single example of this painter devoted to his art with such independence, my destiny as a painter opened out to me."[19]

Claude Monet (shown in this portrait) realized his destiny as an artist once he began painting outdoors.

In the spring of 1859, Monet visited Paris and became enchanted with the paintings that were displayed at the Salon. The next winter, he moved back to the city of his birth and enrolled at an art school called Académie Suisse. He stayed in Paris until he was called up for military service, during which he spent nearly two years in Algeria. After being released from the military, he traveled to the Normandy coast and resumed

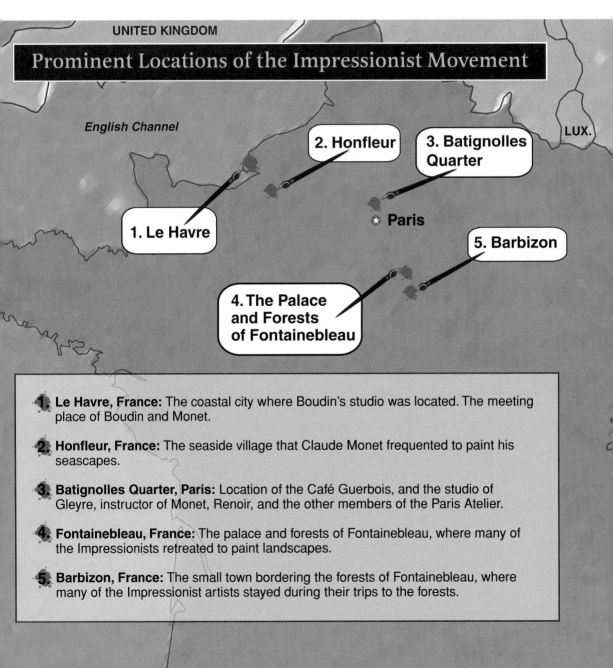

UNITED KINGDOM

Prominent Locations of the Impressionist Movement

English Channel

LUX.

2. Honfleur

3. Batignolles Quarter

1. Le Havre

⭐ **Paris**

5. Barbizon

4. The Palace and Forests of Fontainebleau

1. **Le Havre, France:** The coastal city where Boudin's studio was located. The meeting place of Boudin and Monet.

2. **Honfleur, France:** The seaside village that Claude Monet frequented to paint his seascapes.

3. **Batignolles Quarter, Paris:** Location of the Café Guerbois, and the studio of Gleyre, instructor of Monet, Renoir, and the other members of the Paris Atelier.

4. **Fontainebleau, France:** The palace and forests of Fontainebleau, where many of the Impressionists retreated to paint landscapes.

5. **Barbizon, France:** The small town bordering the forests of Fontainebleau, where many of the Impressionist artists stayed during their trips to the forests.

painting seascapes with Boudin. In November 1862, he returned to Paris and began his studies with Gleyre.

Pierre-Auguste Renoir

Like Monet, Renoir had also shown artistic promise at a young age. Born in February 1841 in the southwestern French city of Limoges, he moved to Paris with his family at the age of three. From the time he was a child, he loved art, and he was constantly drawing and scribbling while he was in school. At the age of fourteen, his family's financial situation forced him to leave school and get a job, and he went to work as an apprentice for a porcelain painter. For the next several years, Renoir painted flowers, tiny portraits, and other delicate designs on plates, lamps, and teapots, and he became more proficient in the art of china painting as time went by. As often as possible, he visited the Louvre, where he tirelessly studied and copied the works of the old masters.

Renoir's love of painting continued to grow, and he yearned for a career as a professional artist. His father, however, could not afford to send him to art school, and neither was he supportive of his son's career choice. He knew that Renoir had artistic talent, but he believed that painting was neither a respectable nor dependable profession.

Yet his son's passion for studying art was obvious, so he asked a trusted associate to look at Renoir's works and determine if he was well suited for an artistic career. After reviewing the paintings, the man urged Renoir's parents to let their son study art and pursue a career as a painter. "I predict a brilliant future for him in the arts," he said, "make sure that you do what I say."[20] In April 1862, Renoir gathered the money he had saved through the years and enrolled in Gleyre's atelier.

Bazille and Sisley

Bazille had been born the same year as Renoir, but his family was much wealthier, having earned a fortune as successful winemakers in the southern French city of Montpellier. Bazille's parents expected that their son would someday become a doctor, and he honored their wishes by studying medicine for three years at the prestigious Montpellier medical academy. In 1862, he moved to Paris to continue his medical education, while also attending morning art classes at Gleyre's atelier. Eventually, Bazille realized that his passion was not medicine, but painting, and he abandoned the idea of becoming a doctor to pursue a career as a full-time artist.

Sisley was also from a wealthy family who was prominent in Parisian society. The son of English parents, he was born in Paris in October 1839 and lived there throughout his childhood. When he was eighteen years old, he went to England to study for a business career, although he had no interest in doing so because his true passion was art. While Sisley was in England, he often visited London art galleries and museums, where he became captivated by the landscape paintings of well-known British artists such as John Constable and Joseph M.W. Turner. In 1862, when he returned to Paris, he informed his parents that he wanted to become a painter, and they supported his decision. By October of that year, Sisley had joined Gleyre's group and was working toward achieving his dream.

New Discoveries

Soon after the four aspiring artists met at the Paris atelier, they were spending much of their time together. They often went for strolls in the Luxembourg Gardens or visited the nearby cafés, where they discussed modern paintings and the artists who were bold enough to create them. One of their favorite topics of discussion was Édouard Manet, whose paintings they had seen at a Paris art gallery. They were all interested in Manet's work, but Monet was positively spellbound by the artist's painting techniques with brushwork and color. Even though Manet was principally a painter of human figures, Monet began to apply some his techniques to his own landscapes.

Monet often talked to the other artists about his passion for landscape painting, and he inspired them to try it for themselves. Within months of their meeting, he had convinced them to accompany him on painting trips to the forest of

Fontainebleau. Like the Barbizon painters before them, the young artists were awed by the beauty of nature, as Wilson describes: "For a young painter . . . it would have been hard to resist the spell of the Forest of Fontainebleau, not only because of its ancient trees, its rocky outcrops and wide avenues . . . but also because of the intimate association with those artists of the previous generation who had opened the eyes of painters and public to the undiscovered beauties of the countryside around Paris."[21]

By the end of 1863, Monet, Renoir, Bazille, and Sisley had grown tired of Gleyre's lessons, which they perceived as dry, stuffy, and overly rigid. Gleyre, in turn, found their youthful eagerness and independence a source of irritation, and he once impatiently asked Renoir if he was just playing at painting in order to amuse himself. Renoir, who loved painting more than anything else in life, replied with complete honesty: "If it didn't amuse me to paint, I wouldn't be doing it."[22] Instead of being inside a studio painting subjects they found boring, the young artists yearned to be outside in the fresh air, studying nature and painting the things they found most interesting. They knew that Gleyre was not fond of landscape painting, as he had once told his students that nature was acceptable only as an element of study and was not a subject worthy of painting—a perspective that sharply contrasted with their own beliefs.

The young artists' tutelage at the atelier came to an end in the spring of 1864. Gleyre, who was suffering from failing eyesight as well as financial problems, closed his studio and retired. Monet, Renoir, Bazille, and Sisley began to devote

The forest of Fontainebleau inspired many landscape painters.

nearly all of their time to painting. They worked in the forest of Fontainebleau, as well as painting seascapes in coastal villages such as Honfleur, on the northern coast of France. Monet especially loved painting at Honfleur, and after completing two seascapes, he submitted them to the Académie for the Salon of 1865.

The Birthplace of Impressionism

During about the same period of time, a section of Paris known as the Batignolles area was growing popular with artists, critics, and everyone else who shared a passion for the arts. In the mid-1860s, a café in the Batignolles area known as Café Guerbois became a favorite hangout for Manet and his fellow artists Camille Pissarro and Paul Cézanne, as well as many others. Edgar Degas, a painter who was known for his fiery personality and razor-sharp tongue, was another regular at the Café Guerbois.

Degas was a Realist artist whose fascination was capturing human movement on canvas, and he often expressed his scorn for landscape painting. He was, however, respectful of artists who were willing to break conventional rules and pursue a more progressive style of art. He especially admired Manet, and the two became friends, although their strong personalities made for a friendship that was often stormy.

The artists who frequented Café Guerbois eventually came to be known as the Batignolles group. During the late afternoons and evenings, they met at the café to have lively, often heated, discussions about anything of interest, from scandalous gossip to art, literature, and painting. Even though they often disagreed heatedly about numerous topics, they all had in common revolutionary ideas about art—and this laid the foundation for the Impressionism movement, as art historian Bernard Denvir explains: "If Impressionism could be said to have a birthplace, the Café Guerbois was it."[23]

Manet was a natural leader at the Café Guerbois gatherings, and along with Degas, typically dominated the discussions, with

the younger artists listening intently and learning from the distinguished painters they had long admired. Eventually, Monet was invited to join the group, and he often took Renoir, Sisley, and Bazille along with him to the Café Guerbois. He later reflected on how valuable the Café Guerbois get-togethers were:

The artists who comprised the Batignolles group exchange ideas in this painting of one of their gatherings.

> Nothing could have been more stimulating than the regular discussions which we used to have there, with their constant clashes of opinion. They kept our wits sharpened, and supplied us with a stock of enthusiasm which lasted us for weeks, and kept us going until the final realization of an idea was accomplished. From them we emerged with a stronger determination and with our thoughts clearer and more sharply defined.[24]

Edgar Degas

Hilaire-Germain-Edgar Degas was born in Paris on July 19, 1834. He showed artistic talent from a young age, and he was encouraged by his family to pursue a career in art. He studied at the Académie's prestigious École des Beaux-Arts, and of all his artistic idols, the classical painter Jean-Auguste-Dominique Ingres was his favorite. Ingres's example influenced Degas to focus on classical draftsmanship that stressed balance and clarity of outline.

Until the 1870s, Degas's main focus was painting contemporary Parisian life such as scenes at horseracing tracks, theaters, cafés, beaches, and music halls. Then he became intrigued with painting female ballet dancers—but it was not their beauty or pretty costumes that interested him. Rather, he was fascinated by human movement. He loved sketching the ballerinas' intricate movements as they warmed up, rehearsed, and whirled around on stage.

When Degas's eyesight began to fail in the 1880s, he became depressed, but he did not turn away from his art. Instead, he devoted his time to sculpture and pastels, which did not require such intense visual ability as oil painting. Degas died in Paris on September 27, 1917.

Manet's Growing Despair

Some of the most spirited discussions at the Café Guerbois revolved around the rigidity of the Académie and the unfairness of the Salon jury. Still, Manet and the other Batignolles artists wanted to be part of the Salon, and they regularly submitted works for the jury's consideration. At the 1865 Salon, two of Renoir's works were accepted, including a portrait of Sisley's father and a painting entitled *Summer Evening*. Both of the seascapes Monet had painted at Honfleur were displayed, as were three paintings by Pissarro and one by Degas. Manet was exhibiting two paintings at the Salon—*Jesus Mocked by the Soldiers* and *Olympia*—and the latter evoked shock and outrage that far surpassed anything he had endured two years before at the Salon des Refusés.

Olympia, which Manet had finished two years before, featured a young woman, completely nude except for a velvet ribbon tied around her neck, lazily stretched out on a bed. Manet had created the painting in the style of Titian's beloved *Venus of Urbino*, but rather than having any appreciation for the comparison, viewers condemned *Olympia*, saying its female subject more closely resembled a prostitute than a goddess. In their eyes, the woman appeared brazen and shameless, and they were infuriated at Manet for what they perceived as cheapening an old master's works. One particularly harsh review stated: "The fact that Olympia has not been pierced and ripped into bits is only due to the security measures . . . where the painting was exhibited. The

Intense hostility toward Manet's *Olympia* overwhelmed and depressed him.

public became more and more indignant, and eventually it was said that Manet had made a joke at the expense of the public."[25]

As was the case whenever Manet was criticized, the hostility toward his painting was unexpected and distressing. He was deeply sensitive about his work and found the insults overwhelming. "Manet lost control and gave in to despair," writes Wilson. "Depressed and disheartened, he wrote to Charles Baudelaire, who had encouraged Manet to send the picture to the Salon . . . 'I would have liked to have had your verdict on my pictures, because all these attacks grate on me, and evidently someone is mistaken.'"[26]

Even after a year had passed, Paris was still buzzing over the *Olympia* scandal and rendering scorn toward the artist who had dared to paint it. When Manet submitted two paintings for the 1866 Salon, the jury rejected them both, which caused him to feel even more dejected and bitter.

"Times Were Getting Harder"

Manet was far from alone in his misery over the Salon jury's continual rejection. The other Batignolles artists were equally distressed, including Renoir. Of the sketch and two paintings he had submitted for the 1866 Salon, the jury accepted only his sketch. Renoir, disgusted by the jury's rejection of his paintings, withdrew the sketch, saying that it was too insignificant to be displayed on its own.

Monet was also struggling. Since the 1865 Salon, only one of his works had been accepted by the jury, and he was having difficulty finding buyers for them. Because his paintings were his only source of income, he was beginning to feel desperate—if he could not sell his works, he had no way of making a living. In 1867, when the jury rejected his prized painting *Women in the Garden*, Monet was filled with despair. His friend Bazille purchased the painting to help keep Monet from sinking further into poverty.

Even though Bazille and some of the other artists did not share Monet's financial situation, they were equally frustrated with the Salon jury's selection process. In addition to rejecting works by Manet and Monet for the 1867 Salon, the jury also rejected works by Renoir, Bazille, Cézanne, Pissarro, and Sisley. In protest, the artists signed a document and sent it to the minister of fine arts, demanding another Salon des Refusés, but French officials declined their request. "Times were getting harder for the avant-garde painters," write art historians Robert Katz and Celestine Dars. "The arbitrariness of the Salon juries who changed their views on what was acceptable from year to year was a cause of intense frustration."[27]

Convinced that drastic measures were necessary, Manet decided to take a bold step. In May 1867, he opened his own art pavilion at the world's fair in Paris, an event called the Exposition Universelle, where he displayed fifty paintings. In a descriptive catalog, Manet described how his frustration had been the catalyst for the independent exhibition:

Renoir's *Lise with a Parasol* won praise but no awards at the Salon de Paris exhibition.

> Monsieur Manet has never wished to protest. On the contrary, the protest, which he never expected, has been directed toward himself; this is because there is a traditional way of teaching form, techniques and appreciation, and because those who have been brought up to believe in those principles will admit no others, a fact which makes them childishly intolerant. Any works which do not conform to those formulae they regard as worthless. They not only arouse criticism, but provoke hostility, even active hostility. To be able to exhibit is the all important thing. . . . By exhibiting, an artist finds friends and allies in his search for recognition.[28]

Photography and Impressionism

Of the many factors that helped usher in the Impressionist movement, none was more significant than the invention of the camera. The miraculous gadget was first introduced in 1839, and within a decade, its use was widespread. Many artists had their own cameras, including most of the Impressionists, because photography simplified their artistic process and helped them create more realistic paintings. For instance, before there were cameras, painters faced the tedious, time-consuming task of manually drawing every detail of an object or scene before they could begin painting it. Cameras allowed them to capture a precise image of their subject on film, and then use the pictures as reference while they painted the image onto their canvases. This was especially exciting for Impressionist artists, who wanted to depict what they actually saw. Paul Cézanne, for one, created his self-portrait in 1866 by copying a photograph of himself, and that same year, Claude Monet used two photographs to paint his famous *Women in the Garden*. Edgar Degas, who used the term "Realist painter" to describe himself more than "Impressionist," was so enchanted with photography's spontaneity that he thought of it as almost magical.

In spite of the time and money Manet had invested, however, the event proved to be a failure for him. Millions of people flocked to the Exposition Universelle, but only a handful of them visited his pavilion.

The following year's Salon was more favorable for Manet, as two paintings he had submitted were accepted by the jury. The same was true for Renoir, Bazille, Pissarro, Sisley, and Degas, whose paintings were also exhibited at the event. One of the paintings at the exhibit was Renoir's *Lise with a Parasol*, which art critic Zacharie Astruc called "enchanting" in his glowing review. "All praise to a joyful canvas made by a painter with a future," Astruc wrote, "an observer who is as responsive to the picturesque as he is careful of reality. This painting deserves to be singled out." Yet in spite of the praise that was showered on Renoir's painting, it did not win even one award, which angered Astruc so much that he used the same review to lash out at the jury: "By an inconceivable error, which I would prefer to think of as ignorance, [*Lise with a Parasol*] has suffered the fate of the rejected work. At the Salon . . . such work stands by its art, its taste and its exceptional character, which command our attention and our study. It was obvious to all the painters, but not to the jury."[29]

Monet also had one painting called *The Steamship* on display at the 1868 Salon. This was little consolation to him, however, since the jury had rejected a seascape that he believed was among his finest works. He became so troubled about his bleak finances that the following June he wrote to Bazille and begged for his help. In a postscript at the end of the letter, Monet implied that he was so desperate he had attempted to commit suicide. "I was so upset yesterday that I was stupid enough to throw myself into the water," he wrote. "Luckily nothing fatal came of it."[30] Although Bazille was growing impatient with Monet's begging, he still came to his friend's aid.

"Irreversible Changes"

The next few years brought even greater disappointment for the struggling artists. Even those who were selected for the Salons of 1869 and 1870 could not fully enjoy the honor, because they were at the mercy of a jury that was biased against them. At one point, they considered forming an independent group that would stage regular exhibitions to rival the Salon, but they gave up on the idea because it would be both expensive and risky. As the artists' anger and disappointment continued to grow, they leaned on each other for strength and tried their best to be positive. Yet they had no way of knowing that they faced even tougher times ahead, as Wilson explains: "By

1870 they had arrived at the point of great discoveries. . . . The Impressionist ranks were formed and ready, but before the battle against mediocrity and prejudice could begin in earnest, external events were to intervene, dispersing the group, and bringing about irreversible changes."[31]

The first of those changes was tragic, and it touched the lives of all the Batignolles artists. In July 1870, a conflict known as the Franco-Prussian War broke out, and within a matter of months, Paris was under siege. The artists were separated as a result of the war; Bazille, Renoir, Manet, and Degas enlisted in the military, while Pissarro and Sisley left for England, joining thousands of other people who fled the country to escape the violence. Monet, who had recently been married, also moved to England with his wife, Camille.

Although the war was short, lasting only ten months, it was both violent and bloody. By the time it was over, nearly one hundred thousand French soldiers were dead—and Jean-Frédéric Bazille was among them. On November 28, 1870, Bazille's life was tragically cut short when he was killed in the line of duty. His death was a horrible blow to the closely knit group of artists who knew him so well and considered him their dear friend.

Growth and Turmoil

The war had temporarily separated the Batignolles artists, but by 1872, most of them had again settled in or around Paris. Despite financial hardships, and especially the tragic death of Bazille, their friendship—and their unified sense of purpose—remained strong.

Their frustration with the artistic establishment had far from diminished, however. The new postwar government was more conservative than the previous administration had been, and this conservatism influenced groups such as the Académie des Beaux-Arts. Thus, the jury had an even stronger bias against artists whose paintings were perceived as radical or too contemporary, as art historian Jean Leymarie writes: "The young painters . . . had nothing to hope for from the Salon, more hostile to them now than ever before."[32]

Assuming that the jury would only snub them, Monet, Pissarro, Degas, and Sisley did not submit any works for the 1872 and 1873 Salons. Renoir was not ready to give up on the Salon, but the two paintings he submitted were both immediately rejected. More frustrated than ever with the jury, he and the other Batignolles artists began pressuring the French government to schedule another Salon des Refusés, and this time their request was granted.

Société Anonyme

The second alternative exhibition opened on May 15, 1873, at a large hall in Paris. Unlike the previous Salon des Refusés, this was a relatively quiet affair, without the scandal of the first exhibit a decade before. The public also showed some interest, with Renoir's enormous painting *Morning Ride in the Bois de Boulogne* receiving especially high praise.

Overall, though, the event was disappointing because very few paintings were sold, which made the artists increasingly anxious about finding outlets where they could sell their works. They began to gather regularly at Renoir's studio, where they revisited the idea they had discussed years before: boycotting the Salon and forming an independent group that would promote artwork sales through their own regular exhibitions. This would give them exposure to large numbers of people, who hopefully would be interested in buying their paintings. In the process, the artists would be sending a clear message to the artistic establishment that they refused to be bullied.

The result of these discussions was the formation of a group called the Société Anonyme des Artistes, Peintres, Sculpteurs, Graveurs, etc. After numerous, and typically heated, debates about how their partnership should be structured, they finally reached an agreement, and by the end of December 1873, they had drafted and signed an official charter. Manet, who had long been their mentor and friend, was adamantly opposed to forming the group and refused to be a part of it. Although he, too, had been a victim of the Salon jury's rejections numerous times, he was convinced that artists should remain in good graces with the Académie and respect its authority. He also believed that painters who refrained from participating in the Salon were admitting defeat, and he urged the others not to let that happen by telling them, "The Salon is the true battlefield."[33]

Jean-Baptiste-Camille Corot, the much-admired Barbizon school painter, shared Manet's viewpoint. Despite the fact that Corot had paved the way toward more contemporary styles of painting, he disagreed with the radical direction taken by

Renoir earned acclaim for *Morning Ride in the Bois de Boulogne* which appeared at the 1873 Salon de Refusés exhibition.

Monet and the other artists in the group. In a letter to Manet, Corot commended him for refusing to be part of the Société Anonyme by writing, "You have done very well to escape from that gang."[34]

Degas's opinion could not have been more different. He often argued with Manet about why it was necessary to form such a group, and he was not happy when Manet refused to be a part of it. Soon after the charter was signed, Degas sent a letter to a friend that described his support for the endeavor and his frustration with Manet. "The Realist movement no longer needs to struggle with the others," he wrote. "It is, it exists and

BERTHE MORISOT

Born on January 14, 1841, in the Parisian suburb of Passy, Berthe Morisot was a member of a wealthy, cultured family. Because she loved art from an early age, her father taught her to draw, and she later pursued formal art instruction. But it was Barbizon school artist Jean-Baptiste-Camille Corot who most influenced Morisot by introducing her to plein air painting. In 1868, she was introduced to Édouard Manet, and the two became close friends. Mesmerized by Morisot's beauty, Manet asked her to pose for his painting *Le Balcon*, the first of many works that featured her. After displaying at the Salon for a number of years, Morisot chose to join the Impressionist movement, and she participated in most of the artists' exhibitions.

Throughout her career, Morisot was forced to cope with an artistic establishment that was dominated by men, and the prejudice she endured was a source of constant frustration. Still, she painted prolifically and regularly displayed her works. After the death of her husband in 1892, she withdrew for a while, painting on her own and spending time with her daughter. Three years later, after being stricken with influenza, Morisot died at the age of fifty-four.

Mesmerized by her beauty, Manet often painted Berthe Morisot.

it must declare itself apart. There must be a Realist Salon; Manet does not understand that."[35]

Another supporter of the independent movement was Berthe Morisot, one of the few acclaimed female artists of the nineteenth century. Having encountered more than her share of prejudice throughout the years, Morisot was well acquainted with the frustrations of her fellow painters. Yet she faced a different sort of bias than they did, as Katz and Dars explain: "The problem for the critics of her day remained the fact that she was a gifted artist and a woman. The two could not easily be reconciled—there was no tradition (acceptable to men) of women in art, and all the critics and judges were men."[36] Morisot was a close friend of Manet's, whom she had met in 1868, and from the very beginning she had been "dazzled by the famous painter notorious for his modernist works and his influence on young artists seeking new experiences of painting."[37] But as much as she admired Manet, she did not share his negativity toward the Société Anonyme. Even though she had maintained a good relationship with the Académie over the years and had displayed paintings in several Salons, she was drawn to the Batignolles artists and shared their commitment to the new artistic movement. This concerned Manet. He knew that Morisot's association with such a controversial group was risky, and he tried to convince her to distance herself from them. She chose, however, to disregard his advice.

The Impressionists

Soon after the Société Anonyme was formed, its members began planning their first independent exhibition. While they were, in effect, competing with the official Salon, their goal was actually not competition; rather, they wanted the freedom to display their paintings without censure, as Denvir writes: "The primary purpose of the organizers was not so much to promote a new style of painting as to escape the constraints of the Salon and to give the artists an opportunity to show their work freely, without the interference of a jury."[38] Just as Manet had refused to be part of the Société Anonyme, he wanted nothing to do with the independent exhibition. The same was true for a number of other painters who feared that being involved would lead to their being shunned as revolutionaries by the Académie.

The Société Anonyme's exhibit opened on April 15, 1874, and was promoted as "the first exhibition of the 'Société anonyme des artistes, peintres, sculpteurs, graveurs.'"[39] It was held at the recently vacated studios of well-known Paris photographer Felix Nadar and featured the works of twenty-nine artists. Monet, who was instrumental in planning the event, displayed seven pastels and five oil paintings, one of which was entitled *Impression, Soleil Levant* (*Impression, Sunrise*). The painting was a seascape of the harbor at Le Havre as it was shrouded in the morning mist, and Monet had painted it using delicate, mosaic-like brushstrokes in light, brilliant colors. There were also six oil paintings on display by Renoir, including *La Loge*, which is described by biographer Lawrence Hanson as "a masterpiece by any standard, the finest picture he had painted."[40]

Degas, who had developed a passion for painting ballet dancers in motion, displayed ten of his works, including a painting entitled *The Dancer*. Also exhibited were two pastels, three watercolors, and four oil paintings by Morisot, five works by Pissarro, two by Sisley, and three by Cézanne, as well as paintings by well-known and established artists not connected with the Batignolles group. These artists had been recruited by Degas because they were highly respected painters and regular exhibitors at the Salon, and he insisted that their presence would lend credibility to the event.

"A Bunch of Young Cranks"

Degas was wrong. Nearly two hundred people attended on the first day, but it quickly became obvious that they were there out of curiosity and a desire to mock the artists, rather than out of a genuine interest in the works on display. The art critics were equally scornful, paying no attention to the paintings by the artists Degas had recruited, and instead focusing their hostilities on the Batignolles artists. Renoir later said that the critics regarded him and his friends as "a bunch of young cranks . . . who wished to attract attention by being silly."[41]

A storm of publicity followed the exhibition. A few positive reviews were published, but they were far outshadowed by harsh criticism—and the naysayers spared no words in vilifying the artists whose works were displayed. Hostile art critics wrote scathing articles, such as an unsigned piece that appeared in the publication *La Patrie*. "Looking at the first rough works—and rough is the right word," the critic wrote, "you simply shrug your shoulders; seeing the next lot, you burst out laughing; but with the last ones you finally get angry. And you are sorry you did not give the [money] you paid to get in to some poor beggar."[42]

None of the participating artists was spared from such attacks. Renowned art critic Louis Leroy wrote a bitingly sarcastic

Monet used delicate brushstrokes in light, brilliant colors for *Impression, Soleil Levant (Impression, Sunrise)*.

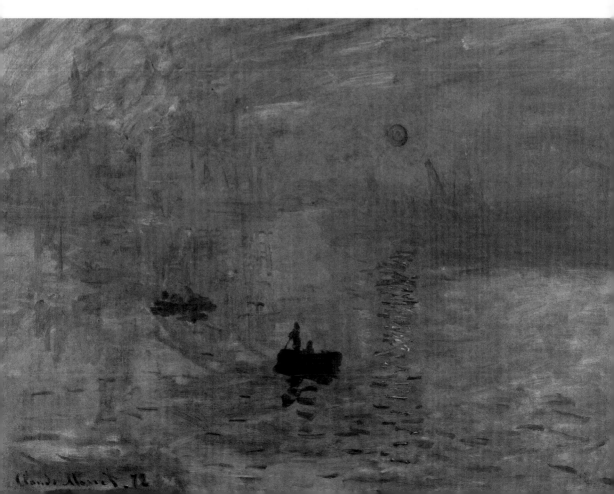

review for the newspaper *Le Charivari*, in which he hurled insults at Pissarro's painting *The Ploughed Field* and mocked Degas's *The Dancer*. But the brunt of his scorn was directed toward Monet's *Impression, Soleil Levant*. "A catastrophe seemed to be imminent," Leroy wrote, "and it was reserved for . . . Monet to contribute the last straw . . . and what freedom, what ease of workmanship! Wallpaper in its embryonic state is more finished than this seascape."[43] An ironic (and unforeseen) result of Leroy's article was its permanent effect on the artistic movement itself. He had entitled his review "Exhibition of the Impressionists," and soon after it was published, everyone from art critics to the general public mockingly referred to the Batignolles artists as "Impressionists."

Monet, Renoir, and the others could never have anticipated such a horrible outcome, nor could they have known that their exhibit would become the laughingstock of Paris. The total attendance at the month-long event was only about thirty-five hundred—a stark contrast with the Salon, which drew tens of thousands of visitors. And because very few works were sold, the exhibition was a financial disaster for the artists. Yet the damage did not end there. The Impressionists had counted on the exhibition to put them in a favorable light with the public, but in fact, the opposite had happened. Their reputations had been tarnished, people were treating them like outcasts, and the artistic establishment had dismissed their paintings as amateur, unfinished, and even outrageous. The artists were stunned, as well as bitterly disappointed.

A Disastrous Experiment

Yet even in the face of public ridicule, they did not give up. They had agreed to band together and create their own style of paintings, and they resolved to keep doing that. At this point, more than ever before, they counted on each other for mutual support and friendship.

The daunting challenge of selling their paintings still loomed, however, and the Impressionists needed to find ways of reaching buyers. In early 1875, Renoir proposed an idea: an auction at which they could display their paintings and put them up for bid. At first, Monet, Morisot, and Sisley were reluctant to participate, because they were still reeling from the public's mockery of their first exhibition. But Renoir managed to convince them that it would be a good way to raise money, and they agreed that such an event might be just the boost they needed.

The auction took place in the spring of 1875 at the Hotel Drouot in Paris, where sales of artwork were often held. Once again Manet refused to participate, but in support of his friends, he sent a letter to influential art critic Albert Wolff and asked him to help promote the event. Wolff responded by writing an article in *Le Figaro*—but it was hardly the positive endorsement that Manet had hoped for. Instead, Wolff spared no words in snidely dismissing the artists' paintings, writing that "the impressionism the Impressionists achieve [is] that of a cat walking on a piano keyboard or a monkey who might have got hold of a box of paints."[44]

Wolff's sarcastic rebuff of the artists' works mirrored the public's reaction, and soon after the auction began, Renoir and the others knew it had been a dreadful mistake. The whole event proved to be a fiasco—people loudly jeered the artists and heckled the auctioneer, as well as pushing and shoving anyone who was brave enough to place a bid. There was such chaos, in fact, that the police were called to control the crowd. The few bids that were placed were so low that they barely covered the cost of the frames, and by the time the auction was over, the Impressionists had endured yet another miserable failure.

Growing Frustration

After so many unsuccessful attempts to sell their paintings, the Impressionists were beginning to doubt that they would ever succeed, and some of them were faced with financial ruin. Sisley, whose family had lost their fortune during the Franco-Prussian War, now depended on his paintings as his only source of income. Monet, whose struggles never seemed to end, was also in serious trouble. Feeling increasingly desperate

In the mid-nineteenth century, when Japan resumed trade with Europe and America, people in Western countries became fascinated with Japanese culture and art. Suddenly, it was fashionable to collect all things Japanese, and the resulting craze became known as Japonisme. Products that were shipped from Japan came wrapped in tissue paper that was printed in colorful Japanese designs, and the Impressionist artists eagerly collected the paper. They found inspiration in the simple yet elegant graphics, bold colors, and asymmetrical compositions (or subjects that were slightly off-center). In 1862 a curio shop called La Porte Chinoise opened near the Louvre in Paris and sold brilliantly colored fans, silk kimonos, china tea sets, lacquered boxes, and a variety of other Japanese artifacts. Before long, the studios of Manet, Degas, Monet, and other Impressionists were graced with these colorful items, which the artists often used as props in their paintings. Monet's 1875 painting entitled *La Japonaise* (*The Japanese Girl*) featured his wife, Camille Monet, dressed in a kimono and holding a Japanese fan.

Camille Monet posed in Japanese dress for this painting by her husband.

over his dwindling finances, he wrote to an art collector and pleaded with the man to buy some of his paintings. In his letter, Monet described the inevitable outcome if his financial situation did not improve. "Once on the street and with nothing left," wrote Monet, "there will only be one thing for me to do: to accept an employment, whatever it may be. That would be a terrible blow."[45]

A sense of despondency was settling over the group. If they were ever going to sell their paintings, they needed to reach people who were interested in buying them. Feeling they were out of options, they decided to hold a second public exhibition, which they knew would be risky—but it was a risk they had no choice but to take.

The second Impressionist exhibition took place from April 11 to May 9, 1876, with just nineteen participating artists, down from twenty-nine at the first exhibit. The site of the event was the Paris gallery of Paul Durand-Ruel, a well-known art collector and dealer who was one of the Impressionists' most loyal supporters. On display were paintings by Monet, Degas, Morisot, Renoir, Pissarro, and Sisley, as well as a new participant, artist Gustave Caillebotte. He had been close friends with Monet and Renoir for years and was such an admirer of their paintings that he had purchased some of them for his own collection.

A Few Positive Signs

The public's reaction to the second Impressionist exhibit was slightly more favorable than previous events, with Degas's *Portraits in the Office*, Caillebotte's *The Floor Strippers*, and Monet's *The Japanese Girl* garnering high praise from spectators. Some art critics wrote positive reviews, but there were others who were as hostile as ever. Wolff, for one, was even more vicious than he had been after the auction a year before, especially in his review of Renoir's painting *Nude in the Sunlight*.

When Renoir had painted the work, he had intentionally avoided depicting his model's skin with a porcelain-like finish, which was the favored technique of traditional painters.

Instead, he sought to capture the effects of natural light and shadow, using warm and cool tones to depict the reflections of the leaves on her skin. But the natural beauty that Renoir had sought to convey in his painting was completely lost on Wolff, who likened the model's skin to a "mass of flesh in the process of decomposition, with green and violet spots which denote the state of complete putrefaction of a corpse."[46]

In addition to attacking Renoir, Wolff took aim at the entire group of artists, including Morisot. He wrote:

> An exhibition has just been opened at Durand-Ruel which allegedly contains paintings. I enter and my horrified eyes behold something terrible. Five or six lunatics, among them a woman, have joined together and exhibited their works. I have seen people rock with laughter in front of these pictures, but my heart bled when I saw them. These would-be artists call themselves revolutionaries, "Impressionists". They take a piece of canvas, colour and brush, daub a few patches of paint on it at random, and sign the whole thing with their name. It is a delusion of the same kind as if the inmates of Bedlam picked up stones . . . and imagined they had found diamonds.[47]

Another Futile Attempt

Yet again the Impressionists were distraught by the hostile reaction of the public and the media. Even though some of their paintings had been sold at the second exhibition, most had not, and the artists acknowledged that they had hosted another failure. This was a difficult realization for them all, but to those who were suffering financially, it was especially devastating. Pissarro, Sisley, and Degas were plagued with financial problems, and Monet's situation had become even worse.

Caillebotte, however, was an extremely wealthy man, and it troubled him to see his friends struggling so hard to survive. Just as he had helped them by buying their paintings in the past, he wanted to help them now. During the winter of 1877,

he invited Monet, Pissarro, Renoir, Sisley, and Degas to his Paris apartment so he could discuss the possibility of holding a third exhibition. Caillebotte offered to fund the entire cost of the event, including paying rent for the studio where it would be held, as well as covering the cost of promotional posters and advertising. The artists accepted his offer and began planning the exhibition for the following April, about a month before the opening of the Salon.

The event took place from April 4 to April 30, 1877, in a spacious five-room apartment in Paris. The eighteen artists who participated displayed a total of 241 paintings, all of which had been carefully arranged to be attractive and appealing to viewers with a wide variety of artistic tastes. There were numerous works displayed by Caillebotte, Monet, Pissarro, Degas, and Sisley, as well as Renoir, whose huge masterpiece *Dancing at the Moulin de la Galette* was given a place of honor. Cézanne, who had chosen not to participate in the previous

Renoir's *Dancing at the Moulin de la Galette* was given a place of honor at a private exhibition but the public scorned it.

year's exhibit, had rejoined the group and was displaying sixteen of his paintings.

Parting of the Ways

To the artists' dismay, the third exhibition was no more successful than the others had been before it. Only a handful of paintings sold, and the reactions of the public and media were every bit as scornful and critical as they had been in the past. The Impressionists, more discouraged than ever, were forced to admit that nothing they tried had succeeded. For years, they had been ruthlessly criticized by the public, battered by the media, and snubbed by the artistic establishment, and they felt beaten down. Renoir, for one, began seriously to question the wisdom of keeping the group together, as his biographer Hanson explains: "As far as he could see the result had been harmful rather than otherwise; they had sold little . . . they had not convinced the public that they were serious; on the contrary they had made themselves a laughingstock."[48]

Because of their obviously bleak situation, Renoir suggested that the artists give up on their boycott of the Salon and try to get back into good graces with the Académie. The others were strongly against such a move, and they urged Renoir to change his mind and stay with them. But when Pissarro, Sisley, and Monet asked him to participate with them in a fourth Impressionist exhibition, he turned them down. After nearly five years of partnership, he had decided to return to the Salon—and this decision was the first of many factors that would change the Impressionist movement forever.

The Turning Point

4

By the end of the 1870s, even though Impressionism was still not accepted by the artistic establishment, it was on its way toward becoming a powerful force in the world of art—yet the very painters who began the movement were drifting apart. Renoir had been the first to break away, followed by Sisley, who decided to resubmit work to the Salon the following year. Monet, too, had begun to distance himself from the others. His wife, Camille, had been diagnosed with cancer, and along with his fear of losing her, he was still trying to cope with serious financial problems. Deeply depressed and bitter over the hopelessness of his life, he had taken Camille to live in the village of Vétheuil, where he isolated himself from the outside world.

After years of friendship, shared goals, and a mutual defiance against the artistic establishment, the Impressionists were starting to go their own separate ways. As much as they may have wanted to keep the group together, they were finding that to be an unrealistic goal, as Wilson writes: "The close unity of purpose that had held the artists together had vanished; from this time on they sought personal solutions and pursued them in increasing isolation."[49]

A Rising Star

When Renoir had chosen to go off on his own, he did not intend to abandon his fellow artists, nor did he want to end their friendship. Since they had formed the Société Anonyme in 1873, he had honored their mutual commitment to exhibit their works independently, even though he was never convinced that boycotting the Salon was the right thing to do. Now, he knew that the only way he could sell his paintings was if he dispelled the artistic establishment's perception of him as a radical and returned to the Salon.

To his dismay, Renoir's close friend Paul Durand-Ruel believed he was betraying the other artists, as well as turning his back on the whole Impressionist cause. Renoir saw Durand-Ruel's accusations as unfair and undeserved, and he addressed them in a letter:

> I will try to explain to you why I submit to the Salon. There are scarcely fifteen collectors able to appreciate a painter outside the Salon. There are eighty thousand who wouldn't buy even a nose if the painter hadn't shown it in the Salon . . . . In a word I don't want to waste my time [protesting] against the Salon. I don't even want to look as though I did. . . . I beg you to plead my cause with my friends. My submissions to the Salon are purely commercial. In any case it is like certain medicines, if they don't do you any good they won't do you harm either.[50]

Even though Renoir's decision was not well received by Durand-Ruel and the Impressionist artists, it proved to be a wise move in his career. The painting he created for the 1878 Salon, *La Tasse de Chocolat* (*The Cup of Chocolate*), was accepted by the jury, and the reaction of the Salon-going public, as well as art critics, was more positive than Renoir had experienced in years. "For the first time," writes Hanson, "the name Renoir began to mean something to the large body of Parisians interested in painting."[51]

In addition to enhancing his credibility, Renoir's return to the Salon availed him of an attractive new assignment from Georges Charpentier, a wealthy, influential French publisher and art collector. Charpentier had first seen Renoir's work in 1875 when he purchased one of his paintings, and he had remained a loyal patron ever since. Upon seeing *La Tasse de Chocolat* at the 1878 Salon, Charpentier commissioned Renoir to paint a portrait of his wife and their two daughters.

For Renoir, this was the ideal opportunity to advance his career and become the highly respected painter he longed to be. Madame Charpentier had a high standing in Parisian society, which Renoir believed would help enhance his credibility with the public, as well as compel the jury to accept his painting and display it prominently at the next year's Salon—and he was correct. His *Madame Charpentier et Ses Enfants* (*Madame Charpentier and Her Children*) was the center of attraction at the 1879 Salon and one of the event's most highly acclaimed works. Spectators gushed over it, and art critics wrote reviews

After years of rejection, Renoir finally received acclaim for *Madame Charpentier et Ses Enfants (Madame Charpentier and Her Children)*.

that hailed Renoir's splendid talent and use of brilliant colors in the painting. Renoir was on his way toward being a star.

"I Don't Have the Strength Anymore"

The other Impressionists, however, were not experiencing the same good fortune. Sisley had submitted two paintings for the 1879 Salon, and both were rejected by the jury, which was a crushing blow for him. His works were not selling well, and his finances were so bleak that he and his family were evicted from their home in the village of Sèvres. Charpentier, one of the few people who had purchased Sisley's paintings over the years, sent the artist some money so he would have a place to live, but Sisley continued to struggle with financial problems.

The same was true of Pissarro, whose paintings were also not selling. Unlike Renoir and Sisley, Pissarro did not want to split away from the Impressionist group and return to the Salon, but his dire financial situation made him fearful about the future. In a letter to a friend, he poured out his despair. "What I suffer at this actual moment is terrible," he wrote, "much more than when I was young, full of enthusiasm and ardour, convinced as I am now of being lost for the future."[52]

Monet's world seemed to be crashing down on him as well. Camille was dying, and in order to be as close to her as possible, he rarely left the house. "Once a common sight on the streets of Paris," writes biographer Charles Merrill Mount, "now he ceased to be seen. . . . He saw no one; letters remained unanswered."[53] Monet's depression was so severe that he found he had no ability to paint—a devastating realization for the artist who was so passionate about his craft.

In early 1879, Caillebotte approached Monet about participating in the fourth Impressionist exhibit, but he had neither the will nor the energy to do so. In an effort to help his friend, Caillebotte gathered twenty-nine of Monet's paintings (including some from his own collection), had them framed, and shipped them to Paris for display at the event. Yet as much as Monet appreciated Caillebotte's kindness, it was little con-

LA VIE MODERNE

In 1879, the French publisher Georges Charpentier released an illustrated magazine called *La Vie Moderne* as a way of helping to promote Impressionist works. The first issue included an announcement of a new art gallery, also called La Vie Moderne, that was located on the same premises as the magazine offices. Charpentier planned to host ongoing exhibits at the gallery while simultaneously describing the artists' works in the magazine. He believed this would increase awareness of the Impressionists' paintings, as well as increase sales. The first public exhibit at La Vie Moderne was in April 1879 and featured a collection of Renoir's pastels, while an event three months later displayed Impressionist drawings. A March 1880 exhibition was much more unusual: It featured numerous decorated ostrich eggs, including several that were painted by Manet, Pissarro, and Renoir. Charpentier hosted a number of other exhibitions at his gallery, and while thousands of people attended, the events were never particularly successful for the Impressionists.

solation at the time. In a letter to art collector Georges deBellio, Monet described his anguish: "I am completely disgusted and demoralized by the existence I have been leading for so long. Each day brings its torments and each day new difficulties arise from which we will never escape . . . I don't have the strength anymore to work under these conditions."[54]

When Camille died in September 1879, Monet was overcome with grief. Throughout her life, he had painted her portrait many times, capturing her beauty, graciousness, and joy of life on canvas. On the morning he found her dead, he could not resist painting her lifeless body one last time—and he felt nothing but disgust that he was able to do so.

Monet painted his beloved wife Camille one last time, on the morning he found her dead.

Claude Monet

Growing Disharmony

After Camille's death, Monet stayed in Vétheuil and worked through his grief alone, as Mount explains: "He saw no one, wrote no letters. He passed his days consumed with a remorse shared only with the bleakness of early winter."[55] Several months went by before Monet felt the first spark of life from within, as though he had finally regained the strength to paint again. In late December, he was once more in front of his easel, capturing images on canvas of the small church beside which his wife had been buried. Throughout the winter he continued to paint, and by the time spring arrived, he was ready once again to try painting for a living. He had, however, made the same decision as Renoir and Sisley: to leave the group and return to the Salon.

Monet had been apart from the other Impressionists for a long time, and when he told them what he planned to do, their reactions were mixed. Caillebotte and Pissarro were unhappy about his leaving, but they understood that he had made the choice he thought was best. Degas did not understand at all—in fact, he was furious. He liked Monet and had a great deal of respect for his work, and the idea that he would abandon the group was unthinkable.

Degas was so angry, in fact, that he refused to speak to Monet, as Hanson explains: "Too critical . . . for his own happiness, he deeply admired few men. Monet had been one of the few, and Degas could not forgive his treachery, as he saw it."[56] Degas freely spoke of his disdain for both Monet and Renoir behind their backs, and questioned Caillebotte about why he would even think of allowing either of the men into his home.

Degas's hostility angered Monet and Renoir. They viewed him as blind to the fact that if the Salon should accept their works, it was a clear indication that the Impressionist cause had triumphed. He, in turn, believed that they were nothing short of traitors.

At the fifth Impressionist exhibition in April 1880, the works of Monet, Renoir, and Sisley were noticeably absent.

Out of the original Impressionist group, only Morisot, Degas, Caillebotte, and Pissarro contributed paintings for display, but there were also works by several newcomers who had been recruited by Degas. One of them was Paul Gauguin, an artist who was very familiar with Impressionist works and had been collecting them for a number of years. Two other new participants were Jean-François Raffaëlli and Mary Cassatt, who were both protégés of Degas. Cassatt was an American artist who was an admirer of Degas and the Impressionists, and because her works were rarely accepted by the Salon, she had long identified with their cause.

Degas and Pissarro, who were instrumental in planning the fifth exhibition, were dismayed by how unsuccessful it was. Attendance was sparse, and art critics were unimpressed by the works that were on display. For those who had positive reactions to the Impressionist exhibits of the past, the new paintings seemed bland and uninteresting, lacking in the freshness and sparkle that had made the Impressionists' works stand out. As a result, the exhibition received poor reviews even by those critics who had written favorable pieces in the past. One of them, Armand Silvestre, had published a glowing review of the artists' first exhibit in 1874, but he had a very different opinion about this event. In the publication, *La Vie Moderne*, Silvestre wrote that there was "no trace of the vision that gave the little school the recognition it deserved in the art of recent years."[57]

New Impressionists

Even though it was Monet's own choice not to participate in the fifth exhibition, he was appalled at Degas for bringing in artists from outside the Impressionist circle to display paintings. During an interview with a journalist, Monet was asked if his absence from the event meant that he no longer considered himself to be an Impressionist. Monet's reply was brusque, and he made no effort to hide his growing frustration with Degas. "Not at all," he answered. "I am still and always intend to be an impressionist . . . but I see only very rarely the men and women who are my colleagues. The little clique has

MARY CASSATT, AMERICAN IMPRESSIONIST

Mary Stevenson Cassatt was born on May 22, 1844, in Allegheny City, Pennsylvania. She began her artistic education at the Pennsylvania Academy of Fine Arts, and then, despite the disapproval of her father, she moved to Paris in 1866 to continue her art studies. In 1874, her painting *Portrait of Madame Cortier* was displayed at the Salon, where it drew the attention of Edgar Degas. Cassatt, in turn, had seen Degas's pastels at a Paris gallery and was captivated by them. She later recalled being so impressed by his work that it changed her life.

As Degas's protégée, Cassatt became a regular contributor to the Impressionist exhibitions from 1879 to 1886. Then her style began to change from a loose Impressionistic technique to a simpler, more straight-forward approach. Eventually, she reached the point where she no longer identified with Impressionism or any other particular artistic movement. Yet she remained loyal to Degas and the other Impressionists and supported them by introducing their works to American collectors, as well as persuading her wealthy friends to buy the paintings. Cassatt died on June 14, 1926, at her country mansion, Château de Beaufresne, near Paris.

become a great club which opens its doors to the first-come dauber [unskilled painter] who knocks."[58]

Renoir's perspective was equally as scornful as Monet's, and his words were just as cutting. Referring to the artist Raffaëlli, whom he considered to be sorely lacking in talent, Renoir bluntly remarked, "Everything in his pictures is rotten, even the grass."[59]

"Disunity into Our Midst"

Renoir and Monet continued to grow more resentful toward Degas. They were tired of his arrogance and were

Gustave Caillebotte (shown in this self-portrait) tried to keep the original group of Impressionist painters together.

convinced that he was largely responsible for the feuding that had torn the group apart. They also believed that he wanted to control the group so he could run things his own way and bring in whatever artists he chose. In an effort to keep the Impressionists together, Caillebotte and Pissarro tried to convince Degas to be more cooperative and stop recruiting his own followers, in the hope that Monet, Renoir, and Sisley might return to the group. Degas refused, however, and the wedge between the artists was driven even deeper.

After what seemed like endless attempts at peacemaking, Caillebotte was tired of it. He was incensed by Degas's stubbornness and volatility, as well as his insistence on discussing the artists' quarrels with people outside their group. He also believed that Degas contributed little to the exhibitions and was unreliable in his support for the events. In January 1881, Caillebotte sent a letter to Pissarro in which he candidly poured out his frustrations and blamed Degas for the group's problems. Caillebotte wrote:

> I should rather like to know whether the public is interested in our individual disputes. Degas introduced disunity into our midst. It is unfortunate for him that he has such an unsatisfactory character. . . . He doesn't hold the prominent place that he ought to according to his talent and, although he will never admit it, he bears the whole world a grudge. . . . One could put together a whole volume of what he has said against Manet, Monet and you. . . . I ask you: isn't it our duty to support each other and to forgive each other's weaknesses rather than to tear each other down? To cap it all, the very one who has talked so much and wanted to do so much has always been the one who has contributed the least. . . . All this depresses me deeply. . . . He has tremendous talent, it is true. I'm the first to proclaim myself his great admirer. But let's stop there. . . . You see, though he has great talent, he doesn't have a great character.[60]

In his letter, Caillebotte urged Pissarro to join him in organizing an Impressionist exhibition that did not include Degas, but Pissarro would not agree. Even though he, too, wanted to keep the original circle of artists together, he was loyal to Degas and refused to side against him. Also, Pissarro had become a mentor to Gauguin and other young artists who often consulted him for advice, and he welcomed these new painters to the Impressionist group. Caillebotte viewed this as disloyalty and felt he had no choice but to split away from Pissarro and Degas. Thus, when the sixth Impressionist exhibition took place in April and May 1881, there were no paintings on display by Caillebotte, just as there were none by Cézanne, Sisley, Monet, or Renoir.

Doubt and Revelation

Although Renoir's paintings were absent from the Impressionist exhibition, two of his works had been accepted by the jury and were on display at the 1881 Salon. Just as he had hoped, he had succeeded in repairing his reputation with the artistic establishment, and in addition to having his works on display at the Salon, his painting sales were going well. In spite of his growing success, however, Renoir felt increasingly restless and uncertain of his own talent and was often plagued with self-doubts, as he later explained: "I had wrung Impressionism dry, and I finally came to the conclusion that I knew neither how to paint nor how to draw. In a word, Impressionism was a blind alley, as far as I was concerned . . . I finally realized that it was too complicated an affair, a kind of painting that made you constantly compromise with yourself."[61]

Later that year, Renoir left for an extended trip to Italy, where he traveled through the cities of Florence, Naples, Rome, and Venice and closely studied the works of great Italian masters such as Titian and Raphael. He was deeply moved by Raphael's massive paintings, known as frescoes, which graced the walls of the Vatican Palace in Rome, and he was equally awed by the ancient Pompeian wall paintings in Naples. Renoir found these and other magnificent works of art

In *The Umbrellas,* Renoir melded crisp, clean characteristics of Italian art with the soft, feathery Impressionist style.

to be tremendously inspiring. For quite some time, he had been questioning the validity of the Impressionist style, as well as having serious doubts about his own talent and ability, and he found just what he needed in Italian art: more precise form, superior composition, and smooth colors and textures—all qualities he felt had been lacking from his own paintings. When Renoir later completed *The Umbrellas,* his changed style was obvious: Two little girls in the painting, as well as the lady behind them, were painted with the soft, feathery brushstrokes characteristic of his Impressionist style, while the rest of the figures on the canvas had a crisper, more linear look.

Renoir left Italy in January 1882 and returned to France with a renewed enthusiasm and purpose. He met up with Cézanne in the south of France, and the two artists began working together, frequently going on landscape painting expeditions in which they captured the beauty of the French countryside at different times of the day. Although they had known each other for years, they had never been particularly close—but when Renoir was stricken with influenza, and then pneumonia, their relationship changed. He was seriously ill, and he stayed with Cézanne and his mother at their home in the town of L'Estaque while they nursed him back to health. It was during this time

Manet had difficulty completing *The Bar at the Folies-Bergère* because of a debilitating disease of the nervous system.

that Renoir saw for the first time "that this supreme artist of his time was also a man with a gentle and kind heart."[62] It took several months for Renoir to recover, and when he was finally well enough to travel, he went to Algiers for a short stay to regain his strength, and then returned home to Paris.

The Death of an Icon

While Renoir was still in southern France, Durand-Ruel took it upon himself to organize the seventh Impressionist exhibition. In an effort to show some semblance of unity among the group, he had collected more than two hundred works from the Impressionist artists. He had tried to convince Manet to participate, but as he always had in the past, he turned down the invitation.

Manet did, however, participate in the Salon of 1882, where he had two paintings on display. One of them, *The Bar at the Folies-Bergère*, pictured a young barmaid who was standing with her back to a mirror, with the sparkling Parisian nightlife reflected in the glass behind her. The painting received exceptionally high praise from spectators and critics and is described by Jennings as "a marvellously grand still-life as well as a sensitive study of the young woman."[63] Yet of all the works Manet had created in his lifetime, this was the most difficult painting for him to complete. For several years, he had been suffering from a debilitating disease of the nervous system, and now his pain was so intense that it was difficult for him even to hold a paintbrush. The disease had progressed rapidly since Manet had been diagnosed several years before, and by the end of 1882, he was paralyzed and unable to walk. On April 20, 1883, his doctors amputated his leg in an effort to save his life. But the operation failed, and ten days later, Édouard Manet died at the age of fifty-one.

His death was a crushing blow to the Impressionist artists who had known and admired him for so many years. Even though he never joined their independent group, nor did he consider himself an Impressionist, it was Manet who had originally inspired the artists with his talent, courage, and strong

MONET'S SERIES PAINTINGS

Claude Monet loved to paint landscapes, and in the 1890s, he began one of his most aggressive undertakings: a multicanvas series that featured various French scenes painted at different times of the day throughout the year. Monet began the paintings in front of his subject, often working on several canvases at the same time, and he spent untold hours reworking the paintings in his studio. His goal was to capture the effects produced by different color and lighting.

The first series, *Meules*, included twenty-five paintings of tall stacks of grain that Monet had painted during the summer, fall, and winter. His *Poplars* series featured a colorful row of tall, sweeping poplar trees in various daylight conditions from spring through fall. To create his *Rouen Cathedral* paintings, Monet spent months studying and painting the Normandy cathedral from across the square, using multicolored brushstrokes to evoke the texture of stone. *Mornings on the Seine* included twenty-one softly colored, delicate paintings that captured the subtleties of early morning light and mist on the river. The *Japanese Bridge* series pictured Monet's beloved gardens at his home in Giverny, France, where he painted more than five hundred canvases, many of which featured his majestic water lilies.

will—and thus, it was he who was largely responsible for the birth of the Impressionist movement. "Manet had been at the centre of their circle, and with his death the circle fragmented,"[64] writes Wilson. For the Impressionists, Manet's death was yet one more sign that the movement they had created was crumbling before their eyes.

The End of an Era

Nowhere was that crumbling more obvious than at the eighth and final Impressionist exhibition, which took place during the spring of 1886. The Exposition de Peinture, as it was called, was nothing like the events of the past. "It was scarcely an Impressionist exhibition at all," says Wilson, "consisting for the most part of Degas's following and the new band of 'divisionists.'"[65] Of the original group, only Degas, Pissarro, and Morisot had paintings on display, while Renoir, Sisley, Monet, Cézanne, and Caillebotte refused to have any part of it. After more than a decade together, the Impressionists, who had once been so committed to each other and to their cause, no longer even resembled the cohesive group they once had been.

Years later, Renoir reflected back on the Impressionist movement, a product of the bold, daring artists who were so passionate about their goals and dreams, and he expressed his sorrow about the partnership's demise. "I had a feeling of being all alone in a desert," he recalled. "We were all one group when we first started out. We stood shoulder to shoulder and we encouraged each other. Then one fine day there was nobody left. The others had gone. It staggers you."[66]

Postimpressionism

About the same time the Impressionist group was breaking up, a new artistic trend was starting to take shape in France. First known as Neoimpressionism, and later Postimpressionism, the style's birth is explained by biographer C. Lewis Hind:

> By 1880 the hard-fought battles of the Impressionists were won: by 1880 Impressionism was a vital force. Manet has been called its genius, Monet its best marksman. What followed? Young men bustled to the front, ill-content, eager to push the new movement further. . . . They desired to express the sensation an object presented to them, never the imitation of it—the significant sensation of a bowl of fruits or pots of flowers . . . the rhythm of a field of corn, the mass of a dusky body . . . the look of a tree. . . . These men say: "What you call beauty is merely a convention; we open new avenues of expression, infinitely more significant than mere beauty."[67]

In essence, Postimpressionism was a natural extension of Impressionism—while also being a rejection of its limitations.

The Postimpressionist artists were influenced and inspired by the Impressionists in that they, too, were determined to follow their own individual styles, rather than conforming to established or expected artistic norms. Artist Georges Seurat once expressed this by saying, "I painted like that because I wanted to get through to something new—a kind of painting that was my own."[68] Also like their predecessors, the Postimpressionists often painted with pure, vibrant colors and used thick applications of paint. But beyond those techniques, the artists' styles were extremely diverse, ranging from paintings with strong outlines and intense colors intended to convey emotions, to works composed entirely of vibrantly colored painted dots.

Bridging the Gap

In addition to a wide difference in artistic styles, there were other qualities that set the Postimpressionist painters apart from the Impressionists. For instance, they wanted to explore artistic techniques that conveyed emotions and intellect, rather than just focusing on the impressions they saw with their eyes. But even more important was their aversion to the Impressionists' casual, naturalistic approach to painting, which, according to the Postimpressionists, sacrificed harmonious design, clarity, order, and balance—all qualities they strongly believed were essential in quality art.

Paul Cézanne, despite being an Impressionist painter, shared that viewpoint. He was loyal to his fellow artists and was friends with both Pissarro and Renoir, but he nevertheless found himself troubled by the direction that Impressionistic art had taken. Cézanne believed that there needed to be a careful balance between total freedom of expression and perfect form, as Gombrich explains:

> He, too, wanted to surrender to his impressions, to paint the forms and colours he saw, not those he knew about or had learned about. . . . The Impressionists were true masters in painting "nature." But was that really enough? Where was that striving for a harmonious

Paul Cézanne (pictured in this self-portrait) was so rarely satisfied with his work that he destroyed thousands of his own paintings.

design, the achievement of solid simplicity and perfect balance which had marked the greatest paintings of the past? The task was to paint "from nature," to make use of the discoveries of the Impressionist masters, and yet to recapture the sense of order and necessity that distinguished the art of [French classical painter] Poussin.[69]

Although Cézanne admired many of the Impressionists' paintings and even thought some were quite brilliant, he also found them to be messy, which to him was simply not tolerable. Cézanne was a true perfectionist—so much so that he was never fully satisfied with anything he painted, and as a result, he rarely signed his works. Throughout his lifetime he destroyed thousands of his own paintings, most of which he had never completed because they were simply not up to his standards.

A Different Impressionist

During the growth of the Impressionist movement, Cézanne often traveled to Paris to visit with his fellow artists, as well as participating in their independent exhibits. But as often as he could, he isolated himself from them, living and working in Aix-en-Provence, more than 400 miles (650km) south of Paris. And while his paintings were Impressionistic, they were curiously different from those of Monet and the other painters in the group. His paintings tended to be dark, with strong, even violent, contrasts of light and shadow.

Although Cézanne enjoyed painting landscapes, his true fascination was with still-life scenes, and over the course of his career, he painted more than two hundred of them in oil and watercolor. As time went by, his artistic techniques became even more meticulous and detailed. "Examine the marks that he makes—small, precise, beautiful, each in place for a reason," writes Cumming. "He only makes marks when he has seen and felt something. He also weaves the marks together to produce a harmony of color and design. Every picture surface trembles with the thrill and anxiety of his intense seeing, feeling, and making."[70]

"Thousands upon Thousands" of Dots

As Cézanne grappled with achieving the right balance between Impressionist techniques and harmonious design and order, Georges Seurat was facing his own artistic challenges. He loved working outdoors painting landscapes, particularly at Honfleur and other French seaport towns. Many of his artistic techniques were undeniably Impressionistic, such as dabbing his canvas with broken colors to suggest shimmering light and movement, but he was not interested in the Impressionist practice of capturing his scenery in a completely natural, impulsive way. Instead, he sought a more scientific approach—creating carefully planned art based on order, reflection, and design.

An important part of this approach for Seurat was a way of controlling colors in order to make them seem more brilliant and powerful than was possible with normal brushstrokes. He had studied the color theory research of scientists Eugène Chevreul, Ogden Nicholas Rood, and Charles Henry, and he was intrigued with their findings: When colors were placed next to each other, from a distance they took on a distinctly different hue. The scientists also found that primary colors arranged in juxtaposition (placed next to each other) created a far more intense and pleasing color than could be achieved by physically mixing paint together on the canvas, as biographer George Slocombe describes: "A red and blue tone in juxtaposition produced the effect of a more brilliant violet on the eye than any violet tint mixed on the palette."[71] Seurat was fascinated by these findings—it was obvious to him that the viewer's eye, more than the artist's palette, was responsible for the mixing of color, and he began to take this scientific approach into consideration whenever he painted.

In 1883, Seurat completed his first major work, *Bathers at Asnières*, a painting he had worked on for almost a year. He intended it for display at the Salon of 1884, but it was not accepted, and he was deeply disappointed at the jury's rejection of a painting that was so important to him. This prompted his

FROM FRIEND TO FOE

One of the most celebrated novelists and critics of the nineteenth century, Émile Zola was a friend to the Impressionists for many years. At a time when the artistic establishment scorned and rejected the artists, Zola staunchly defended them without caring whether he was risking his own credibility in the process. He was closest to Cézanne because they had been friends since they were children. But when Zola released his 1886 novel, *L'Oeuvre*, their lifelong friendship abruptly ended.

L'Oeuvre was the fictional story of a young Parisian artist named Claude Lantier who was frustrated and embittered by his inability to realize his life's goals. Zola depicted him as a painter whose unconventional works drew the fierce opposition of the Salon jury, as well as public mockery, and Cézanne became convinced that Lantier was intended to be him. He saw much of himself in the book, and he could tell that Zola had used intimate knowledge of him as he wrote it. Cézanne was deeply hurt and offended that Zola would violate his privacy in that way. After *L'Oeuvre* was released, he sent an abrupt thank-you note to Zola, and then never saw his old friend again.

decision to join with some of his fellow artists to form the Société des Artistes Indépendants, an organization (much like the Impressionists' Société Anonyme) that was formed to give painters a venue to display their works freely. He participated in the group's first exhibition in 1884, as well as displaying paintings in the last two Impressionist exhibitions—and at the final event, Seurat revealed a painting that, as Katz and Dars write, "caused a storm at the exhibition, and closed the decade of Impressionism with a new form of painting as controversial as that which had begun it."[72]

In *A Sunday on La Grande Jatte* Georges Seurat used a technique called pointillism.

Entitled *A Sunday on La Grande Jatte*, Seurat's painting showed groups of people enjoying a leisurely day on an island in the Seine River. Measuring 7 feet high by 10 feet wide (2m high by 3m wide), it was large enough to dominate the exhibition —but it was not the painting's huge size that most intrigued people. It was Seurat's unprecedented artistic technique, known as pointillism, which involved creating images on canvas by building them with small dots (or points) of pure, unbroken color, placed in close proximity to each other, much like creating a mosaic.

Using the knowledge about color that he had gained through careful study, Seurat theorized that when such a painting was viewed from a distance, the points would blend together so well that they could not be distinguished as individual dots of paint. This would lead to the colors blending in the viewer's eye (or rather, in the viewer's mind) without their losing their intensity or luminosity. Thomas Hoving, former director of New York's Metropolitan Museum of Art, describes the technique:

> Georges Seurat took the Impressionist practice of applying broken colors to suggest shimmering light and movement to a non-naturalistic extreme. Painstakingly, almost obsessively, [he] painted tiny dots and thin slashes of contrasting color side by side— thousands upon thousands of them . . . theorizing that by this stark (and highly abstract) system, the hues would meld and merge and create an optical mixture in the eye of the beholder.[73]

Loyal Followers

Because Seurat had developed such an unique style of art, he was a source of inspiration for a number of other artists, including French painter Paul Signac. An Impressionist artist who had long been an avid admirer of Monet, Caillebotte, Degas, and Manet, Signac had participated in the first exhibition of the Société des Artistes Indépendants. He was captivated by Seurat's talent and his unusual painting techniques, as well as his formalized theories about the application of color. Almost immediately, Signac became so fascinated with pointillism that in 1886 he had stopped painting in his usual style and switched to pointillist methods in all his works. During the summer of 1891, for instance, he created three pointillist-style paintings: *Morning Calm, Evening Calm*, and *Sardine Fishing*. All the paintings were of the sea and fishing scenes, but Signac differentiated them by painting at different times of the day and from varying distances. His carefully contrived compositions, along with color combinations of ocher and orange, and sky blue and violet, were intended to do more than just imitate nature. Like other Postimpressionist artists, Signac wanted to evoke moods and emotions in anyone who looked at his paintings.

Fascinated with the pointillist method, Paul Signac began using it in all of his paintings.

From the time Signac had begun experimenting with pointillism, he was an outspoken proponent of the technique. When Seurat died suddenly at the age of thirty-one, Signac became a major force in spreading the popularity and influence of pointillism.

Like Signac, Camille Pissarro was another Impressionist painter who changed his artistic style in favor of pointillism. Although he was thirty years older than Seurat, he was open to exploring new ways of painting, and he was excited about the younger artist's techniques. It was, in fact, Pissarro who had encouraged Seurat to participate in the final Impressionist exhibition.

Pissarro found Seurat's theories about color to be fascinating, and he was especially intrigued by pointillism, an artistic technique that he considered extraordinary. In a letter to his son, Lucien, Pissarro wrote: "I am totally convinced of the progressive nature of this art and certain that in time it will yield extraordinary results. I do not accept the snobbish judgments of romantic Impressionists in whose interest it is to fight against new tendencies. I accept the challenge, that's all."[74] Soon after Pissarro met Seurat, he began to experiment with pointillistic techniques in his own paintings. In his *View from My Window*, he used pointillism-style brushwork and complementary colors to depict the light of the sky, while in *Haymakers* the mass of painted dots on the canvas was nearly identical to Seurat's pointillist style. Pissarro also sometimes used a combination of Impressionist and pointillist techniques, such as in his painting *Île Lacroix*, in which he used soft gradations of tone and color, delicately balanced with a mass of dotted brushmarks, to convey the effects of fog settling on a river.

As much as Pissarro enjoyed painting in the new style, he grew tired of it by the end of the 1880s. He still had great admiration for pointillism, but he found that he missed the spontaneity of Impressionism. Also, pointillism was such a time-consuming process that Pissarro's production had dropped dramatically. In a letter to a friend, Pissarro wrote: "I am looking for a means of replacing the dots; at the moment I am not achieving what I want. The manner of execution is not swift enough for me and does not respond simultaneously with the feelings within me."[75] Pissarro began to change his artistic techniques again. By 1897, when he painted *Boulevard Montmartre at Night*, his style was again decidedly Impressionistic, with vibrant colors and soft brushwork to

Pissarro reverted to his Impressionist style for *Boulevard Montmartre at Night*.

depict the flickering of streetlights and the reflection of the rain on the pavement.

"Proud to Be Called Barbarian"

Pissarro had long been known as someone who inspired and encouraged young artists, and one of them was Paul Gauguin. A stockbroker by trade, Gauguin had been a fan of Impressionist art since he saw the first independent exhibit in 1874, and he had collected a number of paintings by Monet, Renoir, Sisley, Pissarro, and other Impressionists over the years. He developed such an interest in painting that he began to dabble with it himself in his spare time, with his works very much reflecting the Impressionist influence. When he met Pissarro, the older artist encouraged him to pursue his own individual style, as well as advising him to give up his career and pursue painting full-time. In 1883, at thirty-six years of age, Gauguin took Pissarro's advice and enthusiastically began his new artistic career, recording in his journal, "From now on I will paint every day."[76] Gauguin had great admiration for Pissarro, whom he considered to be his teacher as well as his mentor, and the two often spent time painting together.

It was not long, however, before Gauguin became discontented with the life he was living in France and found himself struggling to find inner peace and harmony. Even though he freely traveled in sophisticated Parisian circles, he somehow felt out of place in Europe, and he yearned for a simpler life. After a journey to the West Indian island of Martinique, he became enthralled with the brilliant colors of the tropical landscape, as well as the natives' uncomplicated way of life. That was a life-changing experience for him—and it radically altered the course of his career.

Yearning to escape to an untouched land of simplicity and beauty, Gauguin sailed to the Pacific island of Tahiti in 1891. There he lived among the native peoples, immersing himself in their customs and habits and painting them in their natural environment. The painting he completed in 1897, entitled

Where Do We Come From? What Are We? Where Are We Going? was Gauguin's most ambitious work, full of symbolic meaning about the confusion, unfairness, and uncertainty of life. He described it in his own words by saying, "I believe that this canvas not only surpasses all the preceding ones but also that I will never do anything better or even similar to it."[77]

The paintings Gauguin created while he was in Tahiti puzzled his fellow artists. To them, the works seemed savage and primitive, radically different from anything he had done in the past. But Gauguin did not care what they thought because he was determined to paint in his own individual way. More than once he unabashedly stated that he was "proud to be called barbarian."[78]

A Tortured Artist

Like Gauguin and the other Postimpressionist painters, Dutch artist Vincent van Gogh was inspired by the Impressionists.

Before he met any of them, most of his early works were painted with thick, rugged brushstrokes and dark, earthy tones and were intended to make a statement about the daily struggles of ordinary, hardworking people. After completing *The Potato Eaters*, for instance, van Gogh wrote to his brother, Theo, that his goal was to "emphasize that those people, eating their potatoes in the lamplight, have dug the earth with those very hands they put in the dish."[79] Without fail, any painting that was created by van Gogh in some way reflected deep meaning, emotion, personal expression, or excitement.

Van Gogh's works began to change in 1886, when he moved to Paris and attended the final Impressionist exhibition. Upon meeting Pissarro, Gauguin, and a few of the other artists, he became fascinated by their focus on light and color. He wanted to bring their techniques into his own paintings, and as

A visitor at New York's Museum of Modern Art contemplates Vincent van Gogh's *Starry Night.*

a result, his palette grew brighter and the tone of his works less serious. He was especially fond of Seurat's pointillism technique and delighted in painting dots and strokes of pure color on his canvas. After years of painting in somber tones, van Gogh became obsessed with the virtually endless possibilities that were open to him. He spent a great deal of time experimenting with such techniques as expressive, swirling brushstrokes, rich textures, and vibrant color combinations.

As much as van Gogh loved painting, however, he was a troubled man. He continuously suffered with bouts of uncontrollable, often debilitating depression, and as a result, he did not like being in the crowded city. In 1888, he moved from Paris to the village of Arles in the south of France, where the weather was warmer and the sun shone brilliantly much of the year, and this cheered him somewhat. He spent his time painting scenes of the French countryside, including wheat fields and poppy fields, boats and cottages at the seashore, and the bright yellow sunflowers that grew nearly everywhere he looked.

Gauguin and van Gogh at Arles

In October 1888, Gauguin traveled to Arles to stay with van Gogh at his cottage. At first the two artists got along well together, painting the countryside and discussing their various artistic techniques. As the weeks passed, however, the weather became colder, and they were forced to spend more time indoors, which strained their relationship. Van Gogh was prone to dark moods and violent temper tantrums, and this contributed to the artists' frequent—and heated—arguments. Van Gogh himself described these disputes as "electric to a degree. We emerge from them sometimes with heads as exhausted as a discharged battery."[80]

On December 23, 1888, van Gogh attacked Gauguin, ostensibly attempting to kill him. The next day, in an impulsive act that art historians have struggled to understand, van Gogh took a sharp razor and slashed off most of his left ear. Determined to escape from the man he considered insane, Gauguin left Arles and never saw van Gogh again.

HENRI DE TOULOUSE-LAUTREC

Henri de Toulouse-Lautrec was born on November 24, 1864, in Albi, France, into a distinguished French family. His education included private schooling and art instruction, and he showed great artistic talent at a young age.

Between the ages of twelve and fourteen, Toulouse-Lautrec broke his left leg and right thighbone. A genetic disorder prevented his legs from growing, so when he was fully mature, he had a man's torso and the legs of a boy. As an adult he was only 4.5 feet (1.5m) tall, and he was thought to be a rather comical figure. Deprived from participating in the activities of someone with a normal body, he began to live solely for his art. He immersed himself in Parisian life, frequenting cabarets, dance halls, and nightclubs, where he sketched the activities around him. Later he expanded his sketches into vividly colored paintings in the Postimpressionist style.

As a result of his fast lifestyle, and perhaps as a way of insulating himself from people's ridicule of his appearance, Toulouse-Lautrec started drinking heavily. In the 1890s, he began treatment for his alcohol abuse, but it did not help him. He died on September 9, 1901, at his château in France.

Van Gogh's mental condition continued to deteriorate, and he found he was gripped with the paralyzing fear of being alone. Filled with despair and hopelessness, he admitted himself to a mental hospital in 1889. While he was at the facility, he painted furiously and obsessively, perhaps in an attempt to fight off the madness that was overtaking him. In just one year, he completed 150 paintings, one of which was his colorful, swirling *Starry Night*, which has been described as "[vibrating] with rockets of burning yellow while planets gyrate like cartwheels. The hills quake and heave, yet the cosmic gold fireworks that swirl against the blue sky are somehow restful."[81] Eventually, van Gogh lost his battle against the demons that had haunted him for years. On July 27, 1890, at thirty-seven years old, he put an end to his misery by taking his own life.

Impressionism, Postimpressionism, and Beyond

Van Gogh, Gauguin, Cézanne, Seurat, and the other Postimpressionists were inspired by Impressionism but wanted to take it to what they perceived was a higher level. Like the Impressionists, their predecessors and mentors, the Postimpressionists were bold, daring, and talented painters who were hungry for new challenges and eager to explore new, unprecedented artistic techniques, even if that meant rejecting the artistic establishment's accepted norms. When these artists were in front of their canvases, they wanted to paint more than just what their eyes saw—they also wanted to convey what their emotions felt and what their intellect knew, and they did this by drawing on science as well as art. "Have I been able to illustrate the intensity of the achievement of these painter pioneers?" Hind challenges the reader. "We who sit at home in ease constructing arm-chair theories can hardly realise their white-hot, fever-tossed mania for expression. . . . But the flame of their lives enables us to understand why [Postimpressionism] has prospered and spread, seeing how fierce were the pioneer fires."[82]

Notes

Introduction: "It Is Shocking . . . Complete Craziness"

1. Michael Wilson, *The Impressionists.* Secaucus, NJ: Chartwell, 1983, p. 8.
2. E.H. Gombrich, *The Story of Art.* Englewood Cliffs, NJ: Prentice Hall, 1972, p. 380.
3. Quoted in William C. Seitz, *Monet.* New York: Abrams, 1982, p. 28.
4. Quoted in Felicitas Tobien, *Impressionism.* Bristol, England: Berghaus Verlag, 1985, p. 13.
5. Gombrich, *The Story of Art*, p. 416.

Chapter 1: The Roots of Impressionism

6. Robert Cumming, *Art.* New York: DK, 2005, p. 266.
7. Quoted in Gombrich, *The Story of Art*, p. 393.
8. Wynford Dewhurst, *Impressionist Painting.* London: George Newnes, 1904, pp. 3–4.
9. Quoted in Robert Katz and Celestine Dars, *The Impressionists.* New York: Barnes & Noble, 1994, p. 21.
10. Guy Jennings, *The Impressionists.* New York: Gallery, 1986, p. 53.
11. Seitz, *Monet*, pp. 14–15.
12. Quoted in Gombrich, *The Story of Art*, p. 404.
13. Quoted in "Eugene Boudin," Paris-Walking-Tours.com. www.paris-walking-tours.com/eugeneboudin.html.
14. Cumming, *Art*, p. 307.
15. Quoted in Bernard Denvir, *The Chronicle of Impressionism.* London: Thames & Hudson, 1993, p. 45.
16. Denvir, *The Chronicle of Impressionism*, p. 27.

Chapter 2: An Artistic Revolution

17. Wilson, *The Impressionists*, p. 32.
18. Quoted in Charles Merrill Mount, *Monet.* New York: Simon & Schuster, 1966, p. 36.
19. Quoted in Seitz, *Monet*, p. 13.
20. Quoted in Lawrence Hanson, *Renoir: The Man, the Painter, and His World.* New York: Dodd, Mead, 1968, p. 28.
21. Wilson, *The Impressionists*, p. 59.
22. Quoted in Hanson, *Renoir*, p. 31

23. Denvir, *The Chronicle of Impressionism*, p. 46.
24. Quoted in Denvir, *The Chronicle of Impressionism*, p. 46.
25. Quoted in Tobien, *Impressionism*, p. 9.
26. Quoted in Wilson, *The Impressionists*, p. 46.
27. Katz and Dars, *The Impressionists*, p. 78.
28. Quoted in Denvir, *The Chronicle of Impressionism*, p. 45.
29. Quoted in Denvir, *The Chronicle of Impressionism*, p. 52.
30. Quoted in Hanson, *Renoir*, p. 85.
31. Wilson, *The Impressionists*, pp. 84–85.

Chapter 3: Growth and Turmoil

32. Jean Leymarie, *Impressionism*, vol. 1. Geneva: Skira, 1955, p. 25.
33. Quoted in Katz and Dars, *The Impressionists*, p. 92.
34. Quoted in Wilson, *The Impressionists*, p. 124.
35. Quoted in Jennings, *The Impressionists*, p. 113.
36. Katz and Dars, *The Impressionists*, p. 274.
37. Jennings, *The Impressionists*, p. 144.
38. Denvir, *The Chronicle of Impressionism*, p. 86.
39. Quoted in "Claude Monet Biography," humanitiesweb.org http://humanitiesweb.org/human.php?s=g &p=c&a=b&ID=35.
40. Hanson, *Renoir*, p. 128.
41. Quoted in Hanson, *Renoir*, p. 128.
42. Quoted in Denvir, *The Chronicle of Impressionism*, p. 89.
43. Quoted in Katz and Dars, *The Impressionists*, p. 10.
44. Quoted in Katz and Dars, *The Impressionists*, p. 98.
45. Quoted in Wilson, *The Impressionists*, p. 128.
46. Quoted in Denvir, *The Chronicle of Impressionism*, p. 97.
47. Quoted in Gombrich, *The Story of Art*, p. 411.
48. Hanson, *Renoir*, p. 174.

Chapter 4: The Turning Point

49. Wilson, *The Impressionists*, p. 150.
50. Quoted in Hanson, *Renoir*, pp. 193–94.
51. Hanson, *Renoir*, p. 176
52. Quoted in Wilson, *The Impressionists*, p. 150.
53. Mount, *Monet*, p. 294.
54. Quoted in Wilson, *The Impressionists*, p. 150.
55. Mount, *Monet*, p. 309.
56. Hanson, *Renoir*, p. 185.
57. Quoted in Denvir, *The Chronicle of Impressionism*, p. 119.
58. Quoted in Mount, *Monet*, pp. 316–17.
59. Quoted in Hanson, *Renoir*, p. 186.
60. Quoted in Denvir, *The Chronicle of Impressionism*, p. 127.
61. Quoted in Rachel Barnes, ed. *Renoir by Renoir*. New York: Knopf, 1990, p. 46.

62. Hanson, *Renoir*, p. 237.

63. Jennings, *The Impressionists*, p. 121.

64. Wilson, *The Impressionists*, p. 172.

65. Wilson, *The Impressionists*, p. 176.

66. Quoted in Wilson, *The Impressionists*, p. 182.

Chapter 5: Postimpressionism

67. C. Lewis Hind, *The Post Impressionists*. London: Methuen, 1911, pp. 9–12.

68. Quoted in John Russell, *Seurat*. New York: Praeger, 1965, p. 11.

69. Gombrich, *The Story of Art*, pp. 428–29.

70. Cumming, *Art*, p. 335.

71. George Slocombe, *Rebels of Art*. New York: American Book-Stratford, 1939, p. 53.

72. Katz and Dars, *The Impressionists*, p. 121.

73. Thomas Hoving, *Art for Dummies.* Foster City, CA: IDG Books Worldwide, 1999, p. 156.

74. Quoted in Katz and Dars, *The Impressionists*, p. 145.

75. Quoted in Jennings, *The Impressionists*, p. 163.

76. Quoted in Jennings, *The Impressionists*, p. 87.

77. Quoted in Jennings, *The Impressionists*, p. 93.

78. Gombrich, *The Story of Art*, p. 439.

79. Quoted in Jennings, *The Impressionists*, p. 232.

80. Quoted in Slocombe, *Rebels of Art*, p. 204.

81. Nicholas Pioch, "Vincent van Gogh —*The Starry Night*," WebMuseum, Paris. www.ibiblio.org/wm/paint/auth/gogh/starry-night.

82. Hind, *The Post Impressionists*, pp. 91–92.

For Further Reading

Books

Bernard Denvir, *The Chronicle of Impressionism*. London: Thames & Hudson, 2000. A highly acclaimed book that covers the history of Impressionism and details of the artists' personal lives. Includes more than four hundred illustrations of paintings, photographs, and drawings.

Robert Katz and Celestine Dars, *The Impressionists*. New York: Barnes & Noble, 1994. An excellent, comprehensive review of the history of Impressionism, as well as the artists who were part of the movement. Includes numerous full-color photographs of paintings by Manet, Monet, Renoir, Degas, Sisley, and other artists from the Impressionist period.

Antony Mason, *Famous Artists: Monet*. Hauppauge, NY: Aladdin, 1994. The life story of the Impressionist Claude Monet, including his boyhood, his years of struggling to make a living as an artist, his role in the Impressionist movement, and his many paintings.

Jude Welton, *Eyewitness: Impressionism*. New York: DK, 2000. A detailed and beautifully illustrated short course on Impressionism, including the artists and their works.

Periodicals

Richard Cork, "Impressions of Despair: Richard Cork Discovers a Darker Monet in the Painter's Long Lament for His Wife," *New Statesman*, September 1, 2003.

Dana Gordon, "Justice to Pissarro," *Commentary*, October 2005.

Robert Hughes, "Still Fresh as Ever," *Time*, March 26, 2001.

Marianne Ruggiero, "Édouard Manet's *Repose*," *School Arts*, October 2001.

Internet Sources

Sabrina Laurent, "The Great Pictorial Movements: Impressionism," *Bohème*, September 2003. www.boheme-magazine.net/php/modules.php?name=News&file=article&sid=66.

Belinda Thomson, "Impressionism (art)," Microsoft Encarta Online Encyclopedia. http://encarta.msn.com/encyclopedia_761553672/Impressionism_(art).html.

Web Sites

American Impressionism and Realism, National Gallery of Art (www.nga.gov/exhibitions/horo_intro.shtm). The online version of the National Gallery's American Impressionist exhibit. Includes beautiful color photos of paintings, biographical information about the artists, and a number of illustrated essays. Information about Postimpressionism can also be found on this site.

Artists by Movement: Impressionism, ArtCyclopedia (www.artcyclopedia.com/history/impressionism.html). An excellent, comprehensive site that includes a chronological listing of the Impressionist painters, biographies, color photos of their works, links to museums where the paintings are housed, and a collection of links to other art-related sites.

Impressionism: Art and Modernity, Metropolitan Museum of Art (www.metmuseum.org/toah/hd/imml/hd_imml.htm). Discusses how Impressionist painting evolved from more traditional forms of art, as well as profiling some of the major artists, their techniques, and their works.

Impressionism.org (www.impressionism.org). An excellent site for anyone who is interested in the history of Impressionism. Features detailed lesson plans that explain Impressionism in clear, understandable terms, as well as an "Experience Impressionism" guided tour.

Index

Picture Credits

Cover: © Christie's Images/ CORBIS

About the Author

Peggy J. Parks holds a bachelor of science degree from Aquinas College in Grand Rapids, Michigan, where she graduated magna cum laude. She is a freelance author who has written more than fifty books for Thomson Gale's Lucent Books, Blackbirch Press, and KidHaven Press imprints. An avid fan of all things related to art and science, her books cover a wide range of topics, including global warming, Mars exploration, the Internet, scientific achievers, famous world landmarks, natural wonders, environmental science, and Middle East conflict. Parks lives in Muskegon, Michigan, a town that she says inspires her writing because of its location on the shores of Lake Michigan.